A NEW WORLD IN OUR HEARTS:
THE FACES OF SPANISH ANARCHISM

A New World in our Hearts

The Faces of Spanish Anarchism

Edited by Albert Meltzer

A new world in our hearts: The faces of Spanish anarchism
   1. Anarchism and anarchists — Spain
   1. Meltzer, Albert
335 ' . 83 ' 0946
ISBN 0 - 932366 - 01 - 5
ISBN 0 - 932366 - 00 - 7 Pbk

Published 1978 by Black Thorn Books,
186 Willow Avenue, Somerville, Mass. 02144
Jacket designed by Les Prince

BLACK THORN BOOKS
186 WILLOW AVENUE · SOMERVILLE, MASSACHUSETTS 02144 · USA

Contents

Contents

"You will be sitting on top of a pile of ruins even if you are victorious."
— "We have always lived in slums and holes in the wall. We will know how to accomodate ourselves for a time. For, you must not forget that we can also build these palaces and cities, here in Spain and in America and everywhere. We, the workers. We can build others to take their place. And better ones. We are not in the least afraid of ruins. We are going to inherit the earth. There is not the slightest doubt about that. The bourgeoisie might blast and ruin its own world before it leaves the stage of history. We carry a new world here, in our hearts, and that world is growing in this minute."

Buenaventura Durruti to Pierre van Passen, August 5, 1936

Introduction

Any attempt to define Spanish anarcho-syndicalist movements of today has to begin with an analysis of Spanish society—however brief that analysis might be.

One is obliged to conclude that the situation today has its roots in the days when Franco was still directly in control. Consequently, it is absurd to think of Francoism as having vanished. What has happened is that there has been a shift away from a dictatorship with its foundations in a range of right wing tendencies (from far right through to social democrats) towards an English-style or Dutch-style constitutional monarchy, with a lingering threat of a backlash from the ultra right who retain quite a bit of support in the Guardia Civil and the Army.

The analogy would fit perfectly, or more or less so, were it not for the fact that Spain's economy, in two ways, lies almost entirely at the mercy of foreigners. For the last seven years or so 44 to 47 per cent of all her foreign trade has been with the Common Market, with the U.S.A. retaining her 15 to 17 per cent . In addition to that, the larger firms are subsidiaries of multinationals, or else they depend on the banking world which itself depends on foreign banks.

For a number of reasons (declining tourism, loss of orders, rising wage bills) the development boom has ground to a halt and for 1978 a minimum increase in the cost of living of 30 per cent is expected. So the government called all the parties together at the Moncloa Palace in Madrid in October 1977, where they all, without a single exception (from the nationalists on the Right to socialists and communists) put their signatures to the "Moncloa Agreement", making public their common ground on such basic matters as a ceiling on wage rises and slow measures to combat unemployment.

Thus did the working class, including those union groups affiliated to the Socialist Party and Communist Party, find itself faced with a fait accompli. There are already signs of widespread discontent among the

ix

unions' rank and file and the commentators of the bourgeois press on the left—like *Triunfo*—are already predicting tactical gains and increased recruitment for the C.N.T. and the extra-parliamentary left (Maoist groups) on account of their opposition to such manipulation from above.

So what does this C.N.T., which its enemies expect to gain victories from in the future, stand for then?

Just as in the past the anarcho-syndicalist union group, the C.N.T., used to comprise a wide panorama from the F.A.I. to feminist groups, naturist and Esperanto circles, so today's C.N.T. also comes in many shapes and sizes. First let's have a look at membership. In theory the various union centres lay claim to astronomical membership: Workers' Commissions (C.P.) 1,500,000: U.G.T. (Socialist Party) around 100,000: U.S.O. (self management from above—!) around 700,000. But it's generally agreed that this is all bluff and none of them, not even the Commissions, is credited with more than 50 per cent of what they claim. The C.N.T., on the other hand, issues only definite figures and, of late, estimated figures, thanks to the rapid growth in membership. A Plenum of Regionals in Madrid at the beginning of September 1977 estimated membership in Catalonia alone at 80,000 (100,000 by now) with smaller groups in the Centre (5,000), the Atlantic coastal areas (5,000), the South (11,000), and Mediterranean coast (15,000) giving a grand total of 116,000 members.

Another thing which differentiates the C.N.T. from the other union groupings, and this is worth underlining, *is that it rejects full time officials out of hand.* Union work has to be done when the day's labour is over. Other union groups already have a total of some hundreds of full-timers. The finance for this comes, apparently, in the form of generous gifts of deutschmarks from the Socialist International, and the coffers of the communist parties. By comparison, the C.N.T. receives a mere trickle of money from Sweden, Italy and, most of all, the Spanish in France, which goes to support the paper *C.N.T.* in Madrid.

The latest factor which might well work to the C.N.T.'s advantage is the question of "trade union heritage", which consists first of all of having the premises, buildings, athenaeums which legally belonged to the unions prior to July 1936 returned: in this way, the U.G.T. and C.G.T. are, little by little, recovering their property and the handing-over of the premises and presses of *Solidaridad Obrera*— a daily which had a circulation of about 50,000, (and this at a time when illiteracy among workers was still extant)—which today are in the hands of the rightwing *Solidaridad Nacional*, is eagerly awaited. Secondly, and more importantly, the term "trade union heritage" also covers, above all, the obligatory contributions made by Spain's workers between 1939 and 1976, in the form of union buildings, health, cultural and sporting organisations, and in the shape of invested capital in an assortment of banks.

The C.N.T.'s greatest problems, though, spring from the fact that it covers a wide range of opinion without having an agreed objective, because of different tendencies locked in combat one with the other (and it looks as if, at times, squabbling behind the scenes consumes far too much time which would be better spent on pressing workers' claims). These tendencies are:—for a belligerent unionism, but only inside the workplace;—for a struggle that is not only a union one but also comprises an ideological fight, equal pay, amnesty for non-political prisoners, eradication of education with diplomas;—or trade union agitation and activism in the working class neighbourhoods, in common with other militants, politicised or not.

Furthermore, there is a wide generation gap between the young and militants who have gone into retirement and generally hark back to the days of the C.N.T. between 1931 and 1937 and don't see how one can be an anarchist *and* smoke and drink (at meetings). On the other hand, the vast majority of members are militants between 18 and 25, many of them having graduated from marxist groups and who therefore despise any sort of group chicanery and are going through a stage in which they reject all coordination for fear of straying from the straight and narrow. In contrast, others of them dream of investing the C.N.T. with Maoist or Trotskyist overtones. The generation of 40 and 50 year olds (more or less contemporaries of Sabaté and the guerillas of 1946-50) is nowhere to be found.

Tactical differences, and distrust of collective action, explain, but they do not excuse the absence of propaganda (in the form of booklets or books) on the part of the C.N.T. and this leaves the bourgeois publishers a free hand or leaves it more or less up to certain individual comrades. Especially striking is the almost non-existence of convincing analyses, and firm stands taken on issues such as unemployment, the economic crisis, the Moncloa agreement. One of the few decisions taken was a message issued prior to the June 1977 elections leaving it up to each voter whether to vote or abstain, which smacks more of opportunism than of anarcho-syndicalism.

The strike at Roca-Gava (a large firm near Barcelona making sanitary equipment) proved crucial, for it exposed the latent "social contract" between the government and the communists and socialists to contain wage levels. There, those strikers who belonged to no trade union grouping were to suffer veritable attacks from the police, plus criticism from all the union groupings. Only when the C.N.T. threw its weight solidly behind the strikers did the attitude of the U.G.T. and U.S.O. begin to change.

As a sure consequence of this stand the C.N.T. has grown in strength in Catalonia from 1900 members in December 1976 to around 100,000 at the present moment. There have been hopeful signs like the affiliation of

Barcelona's transport workers, a group of 500 metalworkers from the SEAT (Fiat) works, officially a stronghold of the Workers' Commissions, and the quite successful November strike by Barcelona filling-station attendants.

Now, the libertarian, anarchist movement is far from identical to the C.N.T.. True, there have been three massive propaganda meetings, near Madrid in March with 35,000 attending, in Valencia in May with 40,000, and in Barcelona on June 2 with some 200,000 present. Nonetheless, there are signs that spectators far outnumber actual members.

The authorities and the political parties (in spite of their electoral success) have dismissed out of hand the extraordinary movement that organises and leads the non-political prisoners in their fight to win humane treatment and an amnesty. Although many anarchists are in their ranks and may be the only ones helping them—it has gone so far that certain prisons have issued statements favouring the C.N.T.—the C.N.T. officially has not done much.

This distrust of what is not purely and traditionally proletarian is reflected in reactions to the libertarian carnival in Barcelona in July. Organised on the request of many C.N.T. members, under the aegis of the Public Spectacles Syndicate and the monthly "independent anarchist" review *Ajoblanco*, this festival attracted around 50,000 participants on a wide spectrum of themes: from theory to music, through feminism, ecology, and sexuality. The bourgeois press—and some comrades, too—seem to recall only some homosexual and sexual freedom demonstrations.

Nevertheless *Ajoblanco* is a legal paper (the C.N.T. has not yet decided to legalize any organ, which only affects circulation and in the long run, the C.N.T. itself) with a circulation of about 90,000 copies. It might be labelled as an anarcho-popular-ecological-sexual magazine, that is for immediate, utter and total freedom for everyone. Which does not prevent it from giving very good reports on May '68 in France, the problems of the government and the C.P. in Italy with the young people, and the independents, and being clear cut about anarchism.

Will the C.N.T. manage to find a focal point and launch a wide front of labour and cultural struggles that will win over even the "independent anarchists"?

For this to become a reality information on the activities of each region and group must circulate. The C.N.T. is full of militants who are carrying out an incredible task costing them a number of hours' militancy each day, with the fatigue and loss of edge that all that implies.

One can only hope that common sense and understanding will remove obstacles like the government's decision to impose union elections which are a means of imposing the Moncloa social contract through the legal operation of the unions in the factories, staffed with leftists this time, not fascists as before.

To counter this, the C.N.T. advocates another sort of fighting organisation: "Coordination must come from departmental assemblies, factory, sector, or area assemblies, and so on, with one or more comrades being nominated who, alongside others from a different section, department or factory, also elected by a workers' assembly, would compose a Delegates Coordinating Committee, an organ of united action which would put the organisation of the workers on a higher plane as regards quality of struggle and combativity in the formulation and solution of their problems. Given that the function of such a body would be to liaise, coordinate and inform, and never to reach decisions: its members would have to present themselves for approval to assemblies on a continuous basis, subject to instant recall and with their position implying no position of privilege beyond that of the other workers." (Decision of the Plenum of Regionals, November 1977).

It is a long, hard fight ahead, but the C.N.T. has already successfully brought off an important task and it has other capacities for growth and strength if only it can respond to the combativity of the workers.

Frank Mintz

Preface

Spain in Today's World

Frequently in the pages of our monthly publication , *Black Flag,* we have
to return to the question of Spain, Spain and yet again Spain. As a result
we stand in danger of being stereotyped as being exclusively devoted to
that country. Yet there is so much of direct relevance to the entire world
in what is happening in the Iberian peninsula. It is not accidental and not
due to some national idiosyncrasy. It solely relates to the persistence of
the libertarian ideal.

The press makes no mention of anarchism in Spain — though note how
quick it is to ascribe "anarchist" to movements elsewhere which are not
such. In the current situation, the newspaper correspondents are, of
course, in touch with their normal contacts — lawyers, journalists, professors, politicians. They have the party combinations at their fingertips.
They can understand a little of what the students are on about too, since
their very dissent is in the main processed by the University, and classes in
"Marxist-Leninism" carefully plan — on an international scale — what is
and what is not the accepted line of protest.

But when it comes to the workers, the journalists turn to the Communist
Party, a well-oiled machine which will give them the answers, and all the
worthy bourgeois journalists, however fascist their papers might be, are
transformed into Comintern agents.

One recalls Heine's story of the old painter who could only paint red
lions and was much in demand by innkeepers: however, one landlord
wanted a blue angel. "It's no use, my friend, asking me to paint a blue
angel — red lions are my speciality, and if I started to paint a blue angel
it would turn out a red lion just the same." It is so easy to have a jour-
nalist's "red lion" — he has the cliches to hand, the Communist Party
menace, the "extremists" and the "moderates", the danger of dictatorship,
the background of Moscow . . . if he started to paint the "blue angel" of
direct responsibility, workers control, internationalism, federalism, it   .
would turn out to be a "red lion" after all. . .

When something happens that cannot be reconciled with Moscow, they fall back on something not quite a red lion and more or less recognisable as a big cat . . . They talk of maoists or Catalan Nationalists as this again is something which can be understood by the Press hispanicists who learned about the Iberian struggle at the bar of El Vino's in Fleet Street.

That is why one does not get much reliable news of what is going on in Spain from the daily press. And perhaps it suits our rulers to see that we are kept in ignorance of that struggle. For in the creation of an anarcho-syndicalist movement over the years there is a challenge to the basic assumptions of authority and the basic principles of accepted institutions.

It is essential to keep the struggle before the trade union movement in this country and to demand help for the Spanish workers in their struggle. Not for their sake. The amount of help that *could* be forthcoming from the British, Australian, Canadian, North American and other English speaking trade union movements is minimal and what has been done is nil. But we must constantly keep before the eyes of all trade unionists what a movement *could* be. We have here a movement subjecting itself to State socialism. Are we so satisfied with it that we wish to impose it on our fellow workers abroad? This is what many people in the Labour Party — as a sop to the Trotskyists, who principally benefit — are proposing. Let us compare our system of organisation step by step with those that have re-emerged in Spain. Comparisons will be very stimulating.

In a typical piece of media misinterpretation, a television programme on Franco repeated the hackneyed story that some people were shot in the Spanish Civil War by the workers "solely for wearing a collar and tie". (This is to ring the changes on an older story about not being able to show calloused hands.) Could they perhaps actually name someone or desist from the story? — if only not to discourage Rael-Brook and Van Heusen from export sales to Spain. In a picture of the late 20's I see Durruti, Ascaso and Jover — the three most "notorious" anarchists of the time — wearing natty cravats and straw hats; the various photographs of the 1930's of well-known anarchist militants show impeccably dressed Valentino types . . . so where did the story arise? Perhaps a reaction to George Orwell's (and others) story that no one wore "bourgeois" ties . . . but after all, the Civil War did start in a Spanish July, which seems to have been overlooked. The tourist of today wants to stroll in those same towns all but naked.

Almost all the older generation of anarchist propagandists in Spain (and elsewhere) wore collars and ties — take a look at Francisco Ferrer Guardia and his comrades. What is a fact, however, is that workers were taken out and every one in ten shot by the Right Wing. Not only in the Civil War: earlier, in the repression in the Asturias, for instance, with the coal miners. What wonder if they in turn shot their persecutors? — whose apologists could only assume it was due to their sartorial splendours! Yet

xvi

it is of this stuff that English speaking readers are expected to judge Spanish anarchism.

In 1955 the well known travel writer S. Mais wrote in "Spanish Holiday":

"The Spaniards all are instinctively individualists and anarchists with a fanaticism that led them centuries ago to cling to their Christian faith in spite of their Moslem churches, and in the late Civil War, led them to destroy the very churches in which they had worshipped.

"I liked enormously the story quoted by Cedric Salter, a great authority on Spain, of the anarchist leader in the Civil War who said to his followers, 'I swear to you that I will never rest until every church in Spain has been burnt to the ground and the power of the churches finally and completely broken. This I solemnly swear in the name of the Father, the Son, and the Holy Ghost. Amen.'"

Very funny. But unfortunately for Mr. Salter (whoever he may be) precisely the same story was told about Pancho Villa who remarked — much more wittily — about the looting of churches, "If the revolution is successful we shall soon find priests to give us absolution." So great an authority is Cedric Salter that he quotes an "Anarchist Leader". One must marvel at the naive belief of S.P.B. Mais that it was anarchism that made the Spaniards Christians — and *he* thinks himself superior to these poor peasants!

It is, of course, easy to interpret the Spanish Anarchist Movement as something exclusively Spanish. This can be done either by the folklorist approach ascribing everything to national character and racial characteristics — dragging in the Moors, paella, flamenco, the Inquisition, seguidillas, mantillas, the expulsion of the Jews, the Conquistadores . . . This is the case with Gerald Brennan in his book "The Spanish Labyrinth", but few writers are exempt — even the Libertarians themselves. In this volume we include essays which reflect this tendency — Jose Peirats, magnificent historian of the labour movement, falls into the trap. There are in Peirats' work a few strands of thought which do not bear close analysis. We may dismiss as naive his belief that State Communism derives from the 'Communist Manifesto' (in which there is no mention of dictatorship and little with which anarchists would disagree) while anarchism derives from "The Conquest of Bread" (a socialistic exposition which does not treat of the differences between State and Free Socialism).

In the essay on "The Origins of the Revolutionary Movement in Spain" this insistence on the special racial or national characteristics of the Spanish workers' movement is repeated many times. One cannot say they have *nothing* to do with it. But not a lot. Such characteristics belong to the workers' movement everywhere. The difference is that in many countries the workers' movement totally changed its character when it ceased to be in the libertarian tradition. By succumbing to reformism or marxism it took on the colouration of the professional classes and lost

xvii

the proletarian. It took on characteristics which were national in that they reflected State attitudes, but it was enough for them to throw off these allegiances to cease to have such attitudes. For instance, the sailors in the Wilhelmshaven Revolt lost totally the "characteristic" obedience and militarism always ascribed to the Germans.

What is the result of this misinterpretation? It can be seen in the trade unions haste to support the UGT or the Communist controlled *Commisiones Obreros* by unions all over the West, spending *our* money, not their own. The UGT receives contributions from Britain, Scandinavia, Germany and America; though it was a union representing only a fraction of the workers before the Civil War and took no part in the Resistance afterwards except that all anti-fascists and workers were persecuted.

The UGT could not have been re-created without this foreign aid, yet, as a union controlled from the top down and based on political participation and collaborationism, not only did it not take part in the Resistance, but one is at a loss to know how it differed from the old official Falangist union (CNS). This too was no more nor less hierarchical than in Britain or France; the rank and file were ignored and the interests of the capitalist State was paramount. For this reason the UGT could not exist clandestinely, not for want of courage.

Much of the money intended for the UGT has gone to Trotskyist groupings of students just as all the money intended for the Comisiones Obreros (as well as that collected in fancy names such as "democratic" fronts) has gone to the Communist Party. Yet the foreign trade union leaders reject these parties in their own countries. They oppose them everywhere but in Spain — partly because (certainly so far as French and British workers' leaders are concerned) as young men they supported the Communist line in Spain and have never realised or wanted to realise it was more disastrous there than in Hungary.

Now the big three are the UGT, the Comisiones Obreros and the USO (which is another relic of the fascist syndicates) and these collectively make up something parallel to the TUC with its policy of State socialism, co-operation with capitalism and the social pact their politicians can define for everyone else. On the other hand, the CNT is a union movement with a long history of struggle, always controlled by its members from the bottom up. It fought for years against the capitalist class and the royalist, feudalist, militarist and capitalist governments. It played the major part in the civil war and as the main workers' organisation and in Catalonia the whole part. Since the Civil War its role in the Resistance has been paramount though not only did it never receive a peseta of support from the rest of the world (unlike nationalist movements receiving heavy subsidies from Communist or Third World governments). It has been denounced as criminal and its members as bandits because it maintained its anti-fascist stand after 1945. Many militants have spent decades in jail for their activities, not to speak of all those who have been killed.

Immediately it was possible to reorganise, the CNT sprang into open existence, to the surprise of foreign observers who took it for granted that it was dead because they always try to write off the contribution of the workers to the struggle, and give credit to the professional classes who thus try to become a leadership. Because the CNT has a libertarian philosophy and is supported by no political party, it does not have a peseta with which to finance itself and must rely on hard-earned pennies of workers or exiles who have, moreover, had to provide for their political prisoners.

The libertarian movement is disadvantaged because while the other parties can spend freely thanks to foreign aid — including the most discreditable sources — during its years of resistance its only way of raising funds for organisation was by bank robberies — for which it was labelled criminal by the very people who had stolen its vast resources. It needs solidarity. After all these years we can still say, Spain's fight is our own.

Albert Meltzer

The Spanish Labour Movement

Frank Mintz

The following article first appeared in **Black Flag** Vol. III, No. 16, December 1974. Frank Mintz is also the author of the authoritative work on self-management during the revolutionary period in the Spanish Civil War. **L'autogestion dans l'Espagne Revolutionnaire** (Belibaste, Paris), an English translation of this title is in progress for Cienfuegos Press and will be published as soon as we have the funds.

THIS IS A BRIEF history of the Spanish republic from the standpoint of the CNT and FAI organisations of the majority of Spanish workers in both the industrial and agricultural sectors (the FAI, *Federacion Anarquista Iberica*, the clandestine anarchist federation, was formed in 1927 with the object of promoting the development of the CNT, the anarcho-syndicalist *Confederacion Nacional del Trabajo*), and an outline of the attitudes of other contemporary political tendencies.

A logical question to ask is why anarchism remained so strong in Spain when it had all but disappeared as a movement in other countries. Indeed to pose such a question is to make the basic Marxist mistake in forgetting the essential fact that real socialist ideas never penetrated the industrial countries at all (with the exceptions of anarcho-syndicalism in the USA up to 1914, anarcho-syndicalism and Marxism in Germany up to 1933) as is clearly shown by the present workers' movements in the USA, Great Britain, Scandinavia and Germany.

In Spain the anarchists were practically alone in employing revolutionary tactics, and from this a soviet historian infers: "Thus, in Spain, anarchism did not restrict itself to utopian propaganda and acts of terrorism. It obtained mass support and achieved a number of practical successes. After half a century of growth this same anarchist tradition has become a weighty material force wielding a great deal of influence."

This influence can be explained by examining the make-up of the CNT and the social and political origins of its membership. The objective of the CNT was libertarian communism as defined by Bakunin and Kropotkin. At the same time the union was open to all workers without political or religious prejudice and, moreover, its leaders came from the working-class itself. These leaders are in evidence from the time of the formation of the First International in Spain (Anselmo Lorenzo and Morago in 1870; Tarrida del Marmol and Sanchez Rosa in 1890; Negre and Buenacasa with the formation of the CNT in 1911; Salvador Segui, Pestana and Peiro after the insurrection of 1917; Durruti, Oliver and Ascaso with the Primo de Rivera dictatorship; Peirats, Vazquez, Mera and Antona in the early years of the Republic and, after the war, the Sabate brothers, Facerias, etc). From 1870 until 1936 there was an uninterrupted flow of successive generations of trained and experienced union men within the Spanish anarchist movement. These sixty years of workers' militancy are still the strength of the CNT. Compare this with 19th century Russia where one finds three separate periods and types of agitation: 1) The *Decembrists* at the beginning of the century; 2) exiles such as Herzen and Bakunin who were converted to socialism; 3) the *Narodniks* or *Populists* who went out among the people but who were themselves the sons and daughters of the bourgeoisie and the nobility, and if one compares it with 20th century Russia where the working-class movement formed its ranks (in practical terms) in the fifteen years between 1905 and 1920, and in which no worker could hold any important position, and where the workers' leaders could be devoured by some petty bourgeois intellectuals such as Lenin, Trotsky and Bukharin etc. Nothing like this happened in Spain. The few leaders from the ranks of the petty bourgeoisie who became involved in the revolutionary movement such as Ricardo Mella prior to 1931, and the doctors Vallina and Puente afterwards, were mostly weak and indecisive.

The second factor which helps explain the strength of the CNT is its three main goals: Direct Action; One Big Union; and Federalism.

Direct Action is the tactic worked out by the French anarcho-syndicalists. It consists of refusing to negotiate directly with the bosses, and in demanding the concession of as many claims as possible. By making the most far reaching demands there remain only two alternatives open to the bosses — accede or oppose. If the workers' demands were rejected by the bosses any show of strength inevitably provoked a chain-reaction among the workers. In 1919 the famous strike at *La Canadiense* showed powerful solidarity in different firms and between different trades. Again, during the republic, there was a strike of telephone employees. The peasants of Ronda, a town in Andalucia, decided to support it and immediately set about cutting all the telegraph wires in the area. That is to say — peasants, for the most part illiterate and acting instinctively, displayed efficiency and solidarity in their action.

The One Big Union, as its name suggests, brought together all the workers within the same company, or in the same area if it were small. The most important effect of this was to unite the wage-earners instead of dividing them into the artificial categories created by the bosses — management executives, technicians, engineers, labourers, etc., — and consequently created a united front when making demands. This created a strength and solidarity far greater than anything the UGT organised on lines similar to the French or German models. It is easy to understand why the CNT strikes were successful. On occasions, when the pressure of the masses was not sufficient in itself, individuals or small affinity groups undertook to strengthen it. Successful strikes led to an influx of new militants which in turn made subsequent strikes more significant as a result of past successes, and drew in yet more militants.

The ideas of Federalism gave greater flexibility of action to the CNT, since each area or local federation could take initiatives without having to consult central committees who might or might not be up to date with the situation in that part of the country. A typical case occured in 1934. The CNT and the UGT disagreed, for reasons that will become clear later, over a particular tactic. In the Asturias, both regional groups had formed an alliance (which shows the influence of anarchist tactics on the UGT), but to the dismay of the local CNT organisation the Felguera federation

2

withheld agreement. Although this may appear contradictory at first sight, it gives some idea of the realities of the relationship between the CNT and the UGT at local level.

An additional aspect of the CNT which is quite remarkable is its internationalism. The CNT never restricted its horizons to syndicalism. Its committee rooms housed literacy classes as well as Ferrer type Free Schools for children throughout the peninsula with financial support from the unions. Militant teachers taught there after working hours, giving classes in Esperanto, vegetarianism, herbal medicine, birth control, female emancipation and general social gatherings. These schools were well-known and were supported by many local and national magazines and journals. In the year 1932, as well as the classic anarchist publications such as *Solidaridad Obrera* (Barcelona daily), *Tierra y Libertad* (Barcelona weekly) *La Tierra* (Madrid), *La Novela Ideal* (monthly) *La Revista Blanca* (Barcelona monthly), *Nosotros* (Valencia monthly), *Redencion* (Alcoy), *Accion* (Cadiz), etc., other anarchist publications made their appearance — *CNT* (Madrid weekly), *Orto* (Valencia), *Solidaridad Proletaria* (Seville), *La Voz del Campesino* (Jerez) etc.

That this militancy had an important cultural side to it was in no way fortuitous. It stood in solid opposition in every way to Roman Catholic culture, from the choice of names for their children — Acracio, Floreal Germinal, Helios, etc., — to the authors they read — Multatuli, Panait, Istrati, Zola etc. The theory and practice of Marxism was presented and attacked for what it was — an ideology which enables the owning class to continue to exploit the workers. Books and pamphlets by Bakunin, Kropotkin, Nettlau, Rocker and so on were published in numerous editions along with the writings of the Russian anarchists Arshinov, Makhno, Voline and other commentators who had seen Bolshevik Russia at first hand — Prieto, Perez Combina, Martin Gudell and Pestana.

However, one must not imagine that the CNT was without weaknesses. The first was the refusal to allow the formation of industrial federations, for fear of bureaucratisation. Had these industrial federations been allowed to develop it would certainly have better prepared the militants with a clearer idea of what was required of them when collectivisation came along. The One Big Union was preserved with its record unblemished, but something was lacking. The propaganda leaflets and books developing the ideas of libertarian communism, the organisation of post-revolutionary society by and for the workers, without a transitory period, foresaw industrial federations liaising among themselves just as did the service groups and agricultural communes, but these were never incorporated into the structure of the union.

A further factor was development without bureaucratisation. One needs to understand that from 1931 the CNT, with about one million members, had only one permanent official — the secretary of the **National Committee**. It goes without saying that all these militants who occupied union posts on national, regional, or local committees did so after their own work, in their own time, and often with their own money. This practice helped discourage careerists, and ensured that those who held office in the union remained in touch with the shop floor and with the rank and file.

3

The number of followers can perhaps be explained by the personal magnetism of certain militants such as Peiro, Vazquez, etc., — workers who had acquired a deeper understanding of the lessons of history and who passed it on to their fellow-workers. From this charismatic influence there grew a power similar to that of a bureaucracy. Peirats recalls that after an insurrection planned and ordered by Durruti and his comrades in the name of the FAI, "someone asked for explanations on behalf of the local federation of the anarchist groups of Barcelona. The reply was that Ascaso, Durruti and Garcia Oliver were not controlled by the FAI, although it was they who had spoken to the meeting in the name of the organisation."

Finally there was the problem of alliances. One can well understand that a social movement, irrespective of its strength and power, can rarely pursue pu ʾly revolutionary tactics. The CNT which was widely split into two separate camps was no exception. On the one side were the *Faistas*, including Durruti and his comrades, who sought to gain from the advent of the republic by declaring for immediate social revolution, and on the other, the *Treintistas*, whose name comes from support for the position taken by thirty officials of the CNT, including Peiro, Pestana, etc., who insisted on allowing the republic a trial period of respectful neutrality. The *Faistas* organised three social insurrections to establish libertarian communism in the villages and towns of Andalucia, Aragon, Valencia and Castille, but all three quickly petered out.

From early 1934 the CNT was split in two and, in addition, severely weakened by the arrests which followed the attempted risings of 1932 and December 1933.

The situation was further aggravated by the election to the *Cortes* of a right-wing majority (partly due to the *Faistas* own campaign of electoral abstention coupled with the failure of the revolutionary movement to take off: "Take over the factories — Social Revolution!"

The actions of other political groupings exerted little influence on the UGT. At no time, for example, did the UGT launch strikes in solidarity with the attempted uprisings by the revolutionary faction of the CNT. The Socialist Party appeared to throw itself into a fervent campaign of revolutionary propaganda, with Largo Caballero, the former Minister of Labour, becoming known as the Spanish Lenin (true inasmuch as he was a political agitator). In fact, Caballero agitated solely for a political deal whereby he could create an armed force which could bring pressure to bear on the right. At no time was an attempted insurrection of the sort undertaken by a section of the CNT ever envisaged by the UGT.

There was, as mentioned earlier, a close CNT-UGT alliance with joint arms caches in the Asturias alone. In October 1934 two insurrections broke out simultaneously in the Asturias and in Catalonia. The CNT took part in the former but was not consulted about the latter. The outcome was rapid. The right refused to negotiate with the socialists and attacked. The Catalan insurrection, led by Catalan separatists, surrendered almost immediately because they had no reserves of heavy armaments. One of the first measures taken by the Catalan authorities on regaining control of the situation was to outlaw the CNT. As for the Asturias, where there was an enormous number of armed workers following the occupation of arms and munitions factories, the area was first isolated, then bombarded into submission.

4

The animosity felt between the socialists of the UGT on the one side and the CNT/FAI on the other deteriorated, except, paradoxically, in the Asturias where UGTers, CNTers and even a minority of communists had fought side by side under the slogan **"Unity among Brother Workers"** — UHP!

With the 1936 elections the left united to win. The CNT discreetly recommended its members to vote and the ballot figures of those elections showed just how strong it was. In the elections of 1933 the left had 3,200,000 voters, 20% of the vote. In 1936 they had over 4,800,000 votes, 35%, representing a gain of over 1,600,000. Of course, the CNT influence, the growth of the electorate, the return to Spain of economic exiles, and the lowering of the voting age, all played a part but a figure of 1,300,000 for the CNT is not unreasonable. The left had gained a slight majority of 1.1% of overall votes cast, but owing to the polling procedure it held a majority of 53 seats. The greatest gains went to the Communist Party — 14 seats to 1 in 1933. Why? The answer is curious. Let us look at the returns: Malaga, 12,900 votes in 1933 to 52,750 in 1936; Cadiz 3,000 to 97,000; Oviedo, 16,830 to 170,500. At this time the Communist Party, according to its own sources, had only a membership of between 17,000 and 30,000, and as a result its propaganda was very limited. But even so, it gained a total of about 1,800,000 votes. The only explanation is that it benefitted from CNT votes, and of 14 Communist Party deputies 13 came from the regions with an anarchist majority.

This political blunder by the CNT in supporting their most stubborn opponents can be explained by the bitterness they felt towards the UGT. In any event the Popular Front was nothing more than a tragic masquerade — the police continued to open fire on workers' meetings, the government took no steps against the *pistoleros* of the right, and the left did little more than embroil itself in polemics, as exemplified by headlines in *Solidaridad Obrera* of July 16, 1936: "Enough! Only fools and agents provocateurs can see any common ground between fascism and anarchism . . may the gentlemen of the Popular Front take note." And, on July 17, 1936: "The counter-revolutionary behaviour and lack of vision of Spanish marxism in times of crises opens the door to fascism."

On July 18, 1936, the right launched a military putsch. The time was well chosen — the left was in disunity, the workers as well as the CNT.

However, despite appearances, the working-class movement, almost wholly CNT inspired resisted grimly winning the day in Catalonia, Asturia and in Madrid. By July 21 two Spains were clearly drawn on the map — one of the left, the other of the right. An unfortunate outcome for the left, particularly the CNT, was the loss of Galicia and parts of Aragon and Andalucia. One immediate effect of the military rising was to oblige the left, diverse in the extreme, ranging from Civil Guard loyal to the Republic, left republicans, socialists, communists and trade-unionists of the UGT and CNT to overlook its disagreements and resist the common enemy. These differences were less obvious at a grass root level among the workers of the UGT/CNT. It was essential to keep the machinery working to provide arms and ammunition for the workers. With that accomplished there was no shortage either of milk or bread. In Barcelona where a week earlier the workers had been carrying on their normal life, a column of volunteer militia, organised by the CNT/FAI, set out for the Aragon front, in covered wagons with first aid for 3,000 men.

From whence came this capacity for self-management? That same June, in France, Simon Weil noted a tremendous apathy among the workers and a sullen defiance of union authority. For us it is unquestionably the structure of the CNT and the internationalist outlook it imbued in its militants which explains this speed of organisation. Even if the lectures, pamphlets and books explaining the ideas of libertarian communism were simplistic they were adequate and, without pretending to offer easy solutions for everything, they convinced the militants of the need to respond quickly to the possibilities of the situation with initiative and creativity.

Let us take some examples. In Barcelona there were several transport companies all of which were amalgamated and collectivised as were several railway companies. It became necessary to resolve problems relating to timetables, liabilities, and spare parts, which was important as they were supplied by foreign manufacturers, as well as new problems of recreation, cultural activities and the problems raised by military transport. One of the first companies to be collectivised — Autobus G — had only 33,000 pesetas in the bank when half a dozen militants took it over, nowhere near enough money to meet its business needs. As had happened throughout Spain in the early days of the rising the bosses took nearly all the assets with them when they fled. They also discovered a card index listing the political affiliations of the workers along with a list of trusted armed men, *pistoleros*. One of the first steps taken by the collective was to get their bearings over the supply of materials, most of which were imported from France, Switzerland, Germany and Czechoslovakia. They decided to become self-sufficient by making as much as possible themselves, and the plant engineers gave this plan full-hearted support. Each engineer was given freedom to study and present plans to the committee and in a short space of time not only were new buses being built, but one section of the shop floor had been turned over to production of armaments for the war effort. Fares were reduced. "We believed we could introduce equal pay for all workers, but we realised that, for a number of reasons, this was not appropriate. Although some wage differentials remained we did manage to abolish many of them." Medical services were improved, showers built, overalls were provided for the mechanics, and loss of pay for two days absence was abolished. Children and pensioners travelled free, and the Autobus G collective gave financial help to the public entertainment collectives in Barcelona, Tortosa and Coll Blanc, and in 1938 they organised relief for a large number of refugees from the Aragon front.

The economic department of Barcelona City Council, under the control of the Communist Comorera (later expelled from the Party and denounced to the Francoist police in 1947 by the Communist Party in the press and radio!), sabotaged the efforts of the collective as far as possible by refusing them permission to import much needed parts from abroad, and by sending armed guards to prevent those parts being stockpiled. Everything possible was done to ensure the collective was made bankrupt and the CNT discredited.

6

The above example allows us to draw certain general conclusions:—

—The right wing was involved in and prepared for the military putsch.

—There was greater unity among workers, technicians and engineers than, for example, occured in Russia where the split was deep and many were exterminated.

—The good sense of the militants who organised the collectives was not blinded by theory or sectarianism. Although men and women did not receive equal pay there was far greater equality than before.

—There was solidarity between the collectives (a factor lacking in Israeli Kibbutzim).

—The above example is typical of the dealings between the various collectives and the Communist Party.

For an example in the agricultural sector let us look at the Villas Viejas project in the province of Cuenca where a landowner had owned a stretch of uncultivated land upon which half a dozen families lived, in hovels, slaving from dawn to dusk to pay him rent. "After one year's collectivisation all the land was under cultivation with twice the number of sheep and goats, a new pig sty and new wheat fields, all supporting fifty-eight families, a school and a library." It would be superfluous to comment on the improvement — suffice it to say that the example is far from unique.

Workers, however, were not encouraged to collectivise and educate themselves by the prevailing climate of opinion. CNT/FAI leaders had not been to the fore in promoting self-education — even at the request of the British consul — and those firms relying on British capital were managed neither by themselves nor from Barcelona. In fact, some anarchists seemed scared by the workers' determination and audacity.

The republicans, for their part, did not use the Bank of Spain's gold reserves to buy arms or the machinery to make them with, in support of the war effort. They even withheld weapons from the front to ensure a powerful internal police and security force. The headlines of Solidaridad Obrera for August 25, 1936, are significant: "In the present time of grave danger weapons must only be used to fight the enemy. All hidden arms to the front!" In Catalonia the separatists proclaimed a forty-hour week and a fifteen per cent wage increase in an attempt to win over the masses from the clutches of the CNT. The CNT responded to this move by pointing out the need to increase production to win the war, to abolish the "English Week", to step up output and increase the number of hours worked in factories under workers' control. However, in spite of the CNT's vociferous denouncements of defaulting and political maneouvering, little was done: "If we had to say clearly all that we *could* have done and which has *not* been done in these past two months — the possibilities we have missed for developing our defence and attack strategy owing to the incapacity and lack of understanding of others with millions in gold lying rotting in Madrid's Bank of Spain — I would be saying too much and therefore would prefer to say nothing at all." The precious gold was handed over to Russia on October 25, 1936 in return for arms used in 1905 and a minimal number of modern weapons — under the strict control of Russian advisers.

Before moving on to the development and problems of self-management in the Spanish revolution we must first look at the growth of the Communist Party, which until now, has remained in the background. In *Mundo Obrera* of October 2, 1934, the following appeared: "The workers can have nothing to do with a Republic such as the one we have at present. The only way out is with the Communist Party, with a workers' and peasants' government — the conquest of power by the urban and rural workers."

A statement issued by the Communist Party to *Pravda* on November 3, 1934 after the Asturian rising stated: "We struggle for workers', peasants', and soldiers' power. The flag of the Soviets has been raised for the first time in the history of Spanish revolution."

But there was no doubting the line taken by the Communist Party at the outbreak of the Civil War. *Mundo Obrera* of July 30 carried the following declaration: "What is actually happening in our country is the bourgeois-democratic revolution. The same one which occured in other countries such as France over a century ago. We Communists stand for a regime of liberty and democracy," and, the following year in a Communist leaflet written by Julio Mateu: "No-one, apart from the Communist Party, in the confusion at the beginning of the civil war, dared to make a stand on behalf of the small landowner."

What was the practical use of collectivisation and workers self-management? Throughout the two and a half years of war the entire war industry was based in factories collectivised by the CNT and the UGT. In many cases they invented original methods of manufacturing arms and explosives. The only financial aid given to the Republic between July 1936 and July 1937 came from the export drive produced by the workers and peasants in the factories and land collectivised by the CNT-UGT. For the first time in history Spanish goods were sold in foreign markets wholesale and on the most favourable terms, whereas before and since the different Spanish firms settled prices between themselves. However, the Minister of Agriculture, the Communist Uribe, soon put paid to that innovation. In 1937-8 all export came under the control of the Communist Party and was sabotaged because the USSR wanted to slow down the progress of the war.

How many collectives were there? Our figures are conservative ones — those of Gaston Leval[*] are the highest. We estimate there were around 1865 collectives covering industry, agriculture, exchange and services. This involved between 1,220,000 and 1,600,000 workers in a working population of 5-6 million, but the division of Spain and the movement of the front makes accuracy difficult.

Who were the collectivists? It should be remembered that there were collectivists from every organisation, including the Communist Party in Catalonia and Aragon (Ariestoles and Cofites), and the POUM (particularly in Raimat in Lerida). At this time the POUM — a coalition of two Marxist groups at the time of the 1936 elections — had very few members, although it had been active since 1930. The Party itself had no dealings with Trotsky, who was critical of it and in C.P. propaganda of past and present (e.g. Vetrov's book *Volonteri svobodi*, Moscow 1972) and the POUM are presented as agents of fascism. Like the Communist Party they were half-hearted when confronted with the movement for collectivisation.

* Gaston Leval   Collectives in the Spanish Revolution, London 1975.

In many cases, such as in Extremadura and Tarragona, collectivisation was non-political, proving that this was the direction Spanish workers wanted the war and revolution to take.

How were the collectives organised? First of all let us examine the collectives of central Spain. By the use of machinery and fertilisers in agriculture, and the rationalisation of production in industry measures were taken to increase output. However, there was also the problem of the lack of certain raw materials, such as cotton, which restricted the textile industry and, during 1938, the heavy bombing which made the electricity supply to industry unreliable. At the same time working conditions improved through the efforts of collective groups in agriculture and re-organisation in industry. Cultural measures were taken such as the setting up of schools and libraries to alleviate the widespread illiteracy. Great progress was also made in the field of health. In Aragon, for example, the doctor lived in the collective and medicine was free and the older workers received a pension — which at present is still far from being administered humanely in Spain and France. Another important point was the almost total absence of ill-feeling. As Kropotkin emphasised in his writings on libertarian communism*, collectivism is for *all*, including even former enemies. This point was respected. In the villages the widows and families of Civil Guards and those killed at the time of the rising were all able to obtain supplies normally from the collective store and to make use of the facilities provided by the community — as in Esplus and Teruel. The Marxists operate very differently and even today families of political prisoners are regarded as inferior citizens. People could leave and re-enter the collectives at will. Seen from outside the collectives organised and liaised between themselves. They organised a federation and set up a common fund to keep a balance between the rich and poor collectives, and between the agricultural, industrial, and service collectives. Thus, for example, the Hairdressers collective in Barcelona financed the buying of machinery, and in particular a water-pump for the village of Asco in Tarragona — a pump which, by the way, is still in operation.

What were the drawbacks and problems of the collectives? The main problem was the short-sightedness of some of the collectives, both agricultural and industrial. They tended to use up their resources willy-nilly, apparently forgetful of the war situation and the political opposition to collectivisation. This led to the development of a neo-capitalism within the collectives which in turn gave rise to a situation where, instead of one boss, some collectives had got to a stage of having many bosses. This problem was overcome by the collectives banding together in industrial unions when threatened by such sanctions as the withholding of necessary materials. However, the problem was soon recognised, faced and corrected.

There was also a shortage of comrades who were capable of book-keeping and there was no collection and collation of the statistics and information needed for vertical and horizontal co-operation. This was due partly to a lack of internal organisational strength, and partly to the amount of time and energy which had to be spent combatting anti-self-management propaganda. The direction collectivisation was taking is difficult to determine because of the war situation. In January 1938 measures were taken

* Peter Kropotkin: His Federalist Ideas, Camillo Berneri, Orkney 1976.

to establish a wage-differential based on a national norm: e.g. a labourer, category 1, received a 20% increase, category 2 a 40% increase, category 3, an auxilliary technician, 1 70% increase and a technical director 100% increase in wages. It is hard to know to what extent this wage structure was followed, but be that as it may, it differs substantially from those of capitalist and socialist countries, even taking into consideration the material advantages of the latter.

There was also a hint of stratification in keeping the libertarian structures controlled from the bottom. The policy was "No factory, workshop, farm, mine, etc., should be shut down unless definite guarantees are given of alternative jobs for the workers."

This explanation, clear as it may seem, gives a completely false picture unless it is seen in conjunction with three over-riding factors. Apart from the daily sabotaging of the collectives which took place from November 1936 onwards, the Catalan law of collectivisation of October 1936 which subordinated all industrial collectives to the hierarchical organisations controlled by the Catalan separatists and the politicians, there was also the attempt by the Communist Party to attack the anarchists militarily during the May Days of 1937. The Communist Party maintains exactly the opposite, but their protestations are dispelled when one notes that the incidents took place *only* in towns where the Communist Party had numerical strength. Lastly, there was the third major anti-collectivist drive by the Communist General Lister's Army Division which, in August 1937, at the height of a Republican offensive and the corn harvest, attacked and destroyed the undefended Aragon collectives, and gave their machinery to the small landowners. As Jose Silva, another communist, is reported as saying: "The result was that all work in the fields was brought to a standstill, and by sowing time not even a quarter of the land for crops had been prepared." Another important fact which belies the C.P. line is that the collectives reformed themselves after Lister had gone, but their former enthusiasm had gone.

It is difficult to draw conclusions from such complex events, but we can learn the following lessons:
History's richest and most profound experiment in collectivisation and self-management is the Spanish experiment. It was anarchist in inspiration, because anarchism alone urges workers to organise themselves from the base upwards, and towards revolution with no transitory political stage.

To have workers' self-management and at the same time remain within the law is impossible. This has already been shown by the experience of the Spartacists, and by the development of the Russian revolution where the workers were, and continue to be, exploited.

The terms "self-management" and "collectivisation" as used in Spain bear no relation to the same terms used today in Algeria, Yugoslavia, France or Britain. Imperialism hampered the course of the revolution. In Spain the role of the USSR and the Spanish Communist Party was to push the anarchists into the front line, discredit and destroy them, to ensure that, after the war, the way would be clear for increasing Communist Party influence within the Spanish labour movement.

Frank Mintz.

(translated by W.Lea & D. Humphries)

10

Further reading on collectivisation: Gaston Leval, *Collectives in the Spanish Revolution*, London 1975, Freedom Press. Sam Dolgoff, *The Anarchist Collectives*, Black Rose/Free Life Editions 1974. Jose Peirats, *The Anarchists in the Spanish Revolution*, Toronto 1977, Solidarity Books. Frank Mintz, *L'autogestion dans l'Espagne revolutionnaire*, Belibaste (English trans. in progress). Cesar Lorenzo, *Les anarchistes espagnoles et le pouvoir, 1868-1969*, Seuil. Daniel Guerin, *L'anarchisme, Ni Dieu ni Maitre*, Gallimard.

Books opposed to collectivisation: Arthur London, *Espagne*, ed. Francais Reunis (Stalinist). Pierre Vilar, *Histoire d'Espagne*.

The Origins of the Revolutionary Movement in Spain

Max Dashar (Helmut Rudiger)

This work first translated from the German, first appeared in English in the U.S.A. in 1934. English editions were published by Coptic Press in 1967 (with slight revisions by the editor Albert Meltzer, to bring it up to 1936) and again in 1972 by Simian Son of Coptic Press.

Two great anti-fascist revolts broke out in Spain in a comparatively short period of time. The anarcho-syndicalist uprising of December 1933, and the protest movement against the Lerroux government in October 1934 which started a widespread mass strike all over Spain, led to numerous encounters between the workers and the armed forces, took the character of a separatist revolt in Catalonia, and developed into a magnificent revolutionary action in the Asturias.

Yet all these struggles were nothing but the climax of the severe social disturbances to which Spain had been uninterruptedly exposed for more than two years. One revolutionary uprising succeeded another. The Iberian peninsula resembled a volcano. Large scale mass actions bore testimony to a revolutionary workers' movement which was not satisfied with the republic. Foreign observers stated these facts time and time again without, however, touching their real core or getting any nearer to an understanding of the truly vital question in Spain. The Spanish revolutionary movement differs radically from the Socialist movements in other countries. Of course, one may draw parallels and make comparisons but that does not exhaust the problem at hand. Only a knowledge of the origin of the revolutionary trends in the Spanish workers' movement and a study of their development, combined with a careful observation of the events from the fall of Primo de Rivera's dictatorship up to the present time (November 1934) will enable us to understand the peculiarity of the Spanish situation, to draw conclusions for the future, and to relate the revolutionary tendencies of the movement in Spain to the revolutionary tendencies of the workers' movement all over the world.

Spanish Independence There is a saying that Africa starts on the other side of the Pyrenees. As a matter of fact, the Pyrenees form a very significant barrier. The ethnologic composition of the Iberian peoples is exceptionally strange. The peninsula has become a veritable melting-pot of races. Throughout centuries war to the hilt has raged uninterruptedly in the different parts of the country. Dark and unknown is the origin of the Keltiberians, the first inhabitants of Iberia. The Basques are perhaps their last survivors. Phoenicians, Greeks and Romans came and mixed with the population; a great number of Jewish immigrants also became part and parcel of the population. The immigrations of the Goths and Vandals ended in Iberia; then the Arabs came from the South, overflowing the country up to the Pyrenees, until they were thrown back, centuries later, by the Christian kings, whose imperialism attracted cultural and racial elements of the Central and South American peoples. The terror of the inquisition initiated by these kings caused the cultural and economic decline of the country which has lasted into the present day and led to the emigration of large parts of the population.

The history, so crowded with radical changes and upheavals, plus the peculiar racial inheritance, accounts for Spanish national psychology. In the fight against the violent and brutal Catholicism that conquered the country after the expulsion of the Arabs, there developed a strong trend towards independence and love of freedom.

Dreaminess, inclination towards fantasy and a distinct feeling for human decency and dignity blend into a peculiar mixture that makes up the character of the Spanish people.

Individualism is their real life element. This has its advantages and disadvantages. The country as a whole is lacking in economic initiative and intellectual productivity; laziness and indolence are a cancer in the body of the nation. As far as civilisation is concerned the country is far behind other European countries. But it has preserved more of its originality. On the other hand, such outdated sentiments as human equality and justice not only find clear expression in the forms of social intercourse, but reach even deeper. The Spaniard may be poor but he does not give up his dignity. Even the beggar does not prostrate himself, but demands his human rights and addresses you as an equal when he asks you for a gift.

This heritage was taken over by the revolutionary workers' movement, which developed in the middle of the last century in Spain. It meant a new departure, the beginning of a progressive development. Its task was to mould into new forms all that was valuable in the national traditions, to stop any tendencies in the wrong direction, and to find its place in the international socialistic movement.

First Revolutionary Influences   The great French Revolution raised the cry for freedom and equality. The young bourgeoisie that soon became the ruling power, interpreted the demand for freedom according to its own class interests — it wanted freedom in commerce and trade, freedom to exploit others. The slogan of equality was soon dropped. Socialism, which rose shortly afterwards, hesitated at first, then developed (in the most important countries) in the opposite direction; it was content with demanding equality, which to many of its adherents was nothing but uniformity, discipline and the mechanical "state-socialism" organisation of all life. Freedom was, as Lenin put it, only a bourgeois prejudice. But it was characteristic of the Spanish workers' movement that it tried from the beginning to defend a socialism of equality and freedom without sacrificing one of the basic demands to the other. It would have been impossible to gather the Spanish proletariat into strongly organised political parties, as has been done in Central Europe, and to submit it to a severe discipline, the way the Socialist Party succeeded in the Germany of the Kaiser and the Weimar Republic. Social democracy and Marxism were able to invade Spain only at a comparatively late date, and until the 1920s, were not deeply rooted among the workers.

Pi y Margall   One of the most important theoreticians of Spanish liberalism, who, at the same time, blazed the trail for libertarian socialism in his country was Pi y Margall. He translated Proudhon into Spanish and thus acquainted the Spanish worker with the great anarchist thinker. Pi y Margall points time and again to the traditional character of the Spanish people, to their love for independence, their dislike of centralism.

"Domestic peace is so hard to attain in Spain because there is no system of administration, of economic and financial policies that would not hurt the interests or views of some locality . . . Many of the old provinces have kept a character and language of their own which distinguish them from the others. Some have preserved their old regional privileges, others have civil laws that contradict entirely the conceptions of family and property in other parts of the country. There are provinces that are both industrial and agrarian in character, others that are purely agrarian . . . Almost all of them have a history and literature of their own. If the same yardstick were to be applied to all, discord would be perpetuated in Spain. Some provinces will flourish through the ruin of others. The unitarian state," Pi y Margall continues, "may perhaps do away with a few small disputes, but, on the other hand, it will destroy the seeds of life that God's own hand has sown in the various districts and regions of the country. The heterogeneousness of the provinces gives life to the whole country but also causes its little quarrels; only **unity of the disparate parts** can do away with this evil — let us therefore organise our country on the basis of a federal republic."

These ideas are just as vital for Spain now (written in Autumn 1934) as when Pi y Margall expressed them. The dictatorial regimentation of Primo de Rivera went on the rocks. In October 1934, the Right started preparations for a new dictatorship, but even the reactionary Catalan bourgeoisie has turned against the too pronounced centralistic tendencies of this regime. The Basque traditionalists and conservatives are turning against the Madrid reactionaries and demanding autonomy for their region. These conflicts can no longer be settled by the bourgeois-capitalist regime in Spain. They will hasten disintegration (*or, as happened, civil war – Ed*). The fight for independence in the capitalist republic has turned into a business rivalry between the various regions, has become part of the economic competitive struggle.

Revolutionary Movement. The situation is entirely different when we turn to the revolutionary movement. Its hope for Spain is a living, co-ordinated libertarian socialism. Only when social equality is attained will the general demand for freedom acquire a meaning, will the free initiative of communities and regions have a real significance for the whole country.

In 1840 the first labour unions were formed in Spain, following the ideas of Margall and Proudhon. In 1868 a decisive step towards a closer union was taken after the visit of Michael Bakunin's friend Fanelli to Madrid and Barcelona, where groups of the International Alliance of the Socialist Democracy, and of the International Workingmen's Association were founded. (The I.W.M.A. existed from 1864). In 1870 all Spanish workers' organisations assembled for their first Congress which had a decidedly anarchist-socialist programme. Nearly all leaders of the new movement supported the federalistic socialism of Pi y Margall but they

14

disagreed with him on the class question. They stood for the active self-liberation of the proletariat, for the social revolution as advocated by the I.W.M.A. (International Workingmen's Association). They differed from Pi y Margall in their attitude towards government methods and parliamentarism; the workers rejected both and progressed to be for organised direct action. They demanded the abolition of the State, which is not only the defender and protector, but also the creator of property and social prejudices. The programme of the Spanish Regional Federation of the I.W.M.A. demanded that:—

"the independent economic organisations of the workers, united on a federal basis, and not subject to any state or political party, take over production, reorganise distribution, and engage in the armed defence of the revolution."

The First Republic In 1870 30,000 workers were members of this organisation; by 1873 there were 300,000. In the same year, they separated from the I.W.M.A. — the First International — after the conflict between Marx and Bakunin and the great international controversy between Marxian state socialism and Bakunin's anti-authoritarian socialism. They belonged for years to the International Organisation of Libertarian Socialist Groups, which had been founded at St. Imier after the Hague congress of the International.

During the first Spanish Republic, 1873-75, the young movement fought valiantly for the cause of the workers, defied the bourgeois federalists and republicans and was suppressed after bloody conflict. The movement continued underground until 1882, when it was reorganised at a convention. Though continually persecuted, and suffering a terrible loss of lives and liberty, the anarchist, later the anarcho-syndicalist movement has continued up to the present day. The Confederacion Nacional del Trabajo (C.N.T; the National Confederation of Labour), founded in 1910, had a membership of 450,000 at the time of the Madrid conference in 1919, and beside that, 350,000 sympathisers had sent delegates. After Primo de Rivera's dictatorship, the organisation was built up again, starting with a membership of nearly 500,000. Since then the movement has suffered inconceivable persecutions and mass imprisonment, has been declared illegal in most parts of the country, even under the Leftist governments, but could not be eradicated. At a regional conference of Andalusia and Estremadura alone, in the summer of 1934, 180,000 members and 80,000 sympathisers sent delegates.

ALLIANCE OF THE SOCIALIST PARTY AND THE BOURGEOISIE AGAINST THE REVOLUTIONARY MOVEMENT

The Spanish Socialist Party was founded in the seventies of the past century after a split in the Madrid group of the I.W.M.A. This group comprised nine members and did not grow larger for quite some time. During the next ten years trade unions were formed which adhered to the conceptions of the Socialist Party; their Union General de los Trabajadores (U.G.T; General Union of Workers) was founded, but developed very slowly. The party tried to take part in the elections of 1882, but it suffered utter, defeat. It is interesting to take a look at its membership after fifty years of active propaganda; in 1915 there were 14,000 members, in 1921 a little over 45,000 in the whole country. In 1926, when Primo's military dictatorship changed into a civilian dictatorship, the Party had six delegates in the Cortes, but they had only won their seats through coalition with the bourgeois republicans during the elections. At this time began the rise of the Socialist Party and the U.G.T. Largo Caballero, leader of the Union, was appointed Counsellor of State in the Ministry of Labour by Primo de Rivera; the Socialist Party worked together with the dictator. The U.G.T. submitted to the laws regulating the organisation and activities of trade unions, sent its delegates to the governmental labour courts of arbitration, and flourished. In the summer of 1931, its members numbered approximately 200,000.

Government-sponsored union. During elections for the legislative Cortes, in June 1931, the Socialist Party again did not come out as an independent class party, but was content with general "republican" slogans. It entered into a new coalition with the various bourgeois "Left" parties and got the largest number of seats in the Constituent Assembly. However, at the November elections in 1933, the number of their deputies was cut in half. In 1931, three socialist ministers entered into the government of the Republic, and there began the golden age of the Socialist Party and its unions (U.G.T.). The U.G.T. became a kind of government-sponsored union and received important privileges; tens of thousands of its functionaires got government jobs. The Socialist Party then made up for its failure in the past sixty years; it became a mass organisation, and through the U.G.T., was able to influence directly the attitude of hundreds of thousands of workers. The cup of democracy was emptied with long draughts — to the bitter dregs.

The dictatorship of Primo de Rivera was to remedy several evils in the country; the increase in the activities of the anarcho-syndicalist C.N.T., frightened the bourgeoisie. The separatism of the regions, especially that of Catalonia, threatened to develop more and more. Besides, the military clique was attacked because of the Moroccan adventure, which has cost the nation tens of thousands of lives. But during the seven years of the dictatorship, neither the revolutionary workers' movement nor the Catalonian regionalism could be destroyed. In 1930 the King had to drop Primo de Rivera and replace him with General Berenguer. In the summer of the same year the bourgeois republicans and the socialists entered into the famous "Pact of San Sebastian" whereby they stipulated the division of the expected loot. The Socialist Party was promised three cabinet posts, which it later awarded to Prieto (Public Works), Caballero (Labour) and De Los Rios (Education). The anarcho-syndicalist Confederacion was also asked to sign the pact and it was likewise offered ministries. It declined, but said that it would fight for democratic liberties on the side of the people, without taking part in a bourgeois republic. And just this happened.

The young republic fell into the hands of a bourgeois-socialist coalition, which, except for the short presidency of Alcala Zamoras, between the proclamation of the Republic in April 1931 and the reconstruction of the Cabinet in October that year, ruled the country for two years under Manuel Azana. The government sought to solve several problems. The first was that of agrarian reform.

Agrarian Reform. Spain is a rural country. There are only two millions of industrial workers — their ranks, large during the period of the First World War because of war profits in industry, had been sharply reduced by post-war crises; while the number of farm labourers in the country amounted to over four and a half million. The oldest and largest industry is the textile industry, mainly located in Catalonia. The central parts of the country, as well as Andalusia and Estremadura, are in the hands of big land owners. Valencia and the North were settled mostly by small land-owners, while in Catalonia the land was generally leased to small tenants (wine growers). The rural workers lived since ancient times in indescribable misery. They seldom had enough to eat. The greatest part of the year they were unemployed, and during the harvest months they worked under police supervision. The situation of most of the landowners was not a great deal different. 1934 statistics divide the landed proprietor into the following groups: 845,000 small landowners earning only one peseta per day, either because they had not enough land or because it was very poor. Some 160,000 proprietors had attained economic independence to a certain degree, because the whole family worked very hard and reduced its wants to a minimum. The number of well-to-do peasants was estimated at 10,000, but most of the soil was in the hands of 9,000 landowners who squandered its profits in the cities but never did a stroke of work.

The Church Another important problem that faced the new State was the separation from the Church. The Catholic clergy was gobbling up an enormous part of the budget. Schools were completely under their influence. Nothing was done for a free, universal-educational system; nearly three-quarters of the population were illiterate. Any attempt to organise a secular school system had been blocked by the Church. At the beginning of the century, the anarchist Francisco Ferrer had succeeded in creating a free school organisation, which soon began to establish small free school groups all over the country. His organisation was outlawed; the schools were closed. When the great anarcho-syndicalist uprising against the Moroccan War broke out in Barcelona in 1909, Ferrer was imprisoned and executed as one of the instigators of the movement, though he had nothing to do with it; the Catholic Church in Spain was never loathe to commit such crimes. Now, finally, its fateful political power was to be broken.

Failure of the Republic As to social reforms, the Azana government aimed to turn Spain into a copy of the Weimar Republic in Germany. Wages and working hours were to be regulated by government bodies, strikes and direct action of the workers were to be looked upon as outlived remnants dating from the infancy of the social struggle and were to be abolished as such. The government also planned to introduce obligatory social and unemployment insurance, according to the Central European pattern.

But the new regime failed miserably. The Azana-Prieto-Caballero government did not fulfil any of the many promises that had helped them to power. However, their policies were such as to help the waiting reactionaries to power! Gil Robles began to enjoy in leisurely fashion the fruits of the republican policy of coalition. Aside from that, the Spanish revolution was a thorough anachronism; a "democratic" revolution in 1931 when the world was ready to scrap democratic illusions, and a last attempt to save the capitalist system by turning backward, towards state absolutism! This experiment could not end any other way than it actually did. As to the revolutionary workers' movement, it was not able, in 1931, to inspire a decisive part of the masses to push the revolution forward, and so the Socialists and U.G.T., rose to power. This power they used to defeat their revolutionary competitors in the workers' movement and to widen the breach among the Spanish workers, by resorting to every means of legislation and governmental violence. The revolutionary labour movement was systematically weakened and destroyed while at the same time the reformist law-abiding workers were influenced against direct action. The results of the policy were the events of October 1934.

Only a small part of the programme of the Azana government was put into effect during its two years in office, but none of it was in favour of the working class.

The agrarian reform did not take any steps towards abolishing the large estates, but made provisions to gradually divide certain large tracts into small properties. The capital value of the land was to be credited to the former owners, and the new small landowners were to become economically dependent from the very beginning by having to pay interest to the big landholders.

Every vestige of socialist tendency was abandoned. Before the agrarian law was carried out, it was emasculated by numerous "reforms" of the law itself. The later governments, succeeding the socialist-republican coalition, gradually divested the whole fabric of agrarian laws of its already innocuous contents.

The separation of Church and State was partly carried through. A number of members of the Jesuit Order were expelled, but the Order itself continued to exist. Laws were promulgated for the secularisation of education, all religious educational institutions were to abandon their ecclesiastical character. But the religious orders started to form private capitalistic organisations that took over the educational institutions. Thus, through many subterfuges the Church maintained its influence in the schools. The State did not have money enough to carry out its own programme for building schools. Instead it created a new shock police, the Guardia de Asalto, for the special purpose of suppressing the anarcho-syndicalists. The military budget of the Republic was greater than that of the monarchy, the fight against illiteracy remained a dead letter.

The new Minister of Labour, Largo Caballero, became very active. His main achievement was the Law of April 8th 1932, through which he intended to solve the problem of labour unions; all workers' organisations had to submit to a certain State control; they had to take part in the State "Labour Courts of Arbitration" to which all labour conflicts were to be submitted; and finally, the date of strikes had to be announced in advance. The Socialist U.G.T., submitted, of course, to all those terms and put its members into the vacancies of the Jurados Mixtos (Labour Arbitration Courts). Not so the C.N.T. They did not recognise the law and did not submit to it.

Attack on the Anarchists According to the letter of the law, the C.N.T., should therefore have been dissolved automatically, but the government did not dare take this step. The anarcho-syndicalist organisation was, however, hampered in its activities; its militant members were arrested, and its headquarters closed where ever possible. The C.N.T., and its great social revolutionary mass movement all over the country were slandered as never before. The militant workers of the Confederacion and the Anarchist Federation of Iberia (F.A.I.), were branded as "bandits with a membership card" by the Socialists. Towards the end of the Azana Government, in the summer of 1933, a new attack was prepared against the revolutionary labour movement. News items in the Press, for which neither the police nor the Ministry of the Interior wanted to assume responsibility, announced the discovery of a far-reaching "anarchist-monarchist" plot against the Republic. The Government ordered new mass arrests. The example of an Andalusian town where the Chief of Police received orders from Madrid to arrest a certain number of leading monarchists and the same number of anarchists (!) shows clearly how this "plot" was discovered. Orders were carried out. One of the best-known monarchists of the town, having been on a trip, reported to the police voluntarily upon his return. But they declined to arrest him, stating that they had already the desired number of monarchists!

Police Power The legislative activity of the Socialist Party and the bourgeois republicans reached its highest point in the new laws for public safety and against vagrancy. The former offered the police a much desired power to proceed against the workers and to suppress any move of the revolutionary organisations. Leading anarchist militants were to be subjected to the law against vagrancy under which they would finally land in the concentration camp. But this attempt had to be abandoned. The law for public safety which had previously served to sap the vitality from anarcho-syndicalism, was used against the Socialist organisations themselves after the Socialist Party was eliminated from the government of the Republic. After the fall of Azana and the Socialists, the governments of the republic used to justify their various acts of suppression against the workers by referring to the legislation that had been created with socialist co-operation; in questions of the rights of labour they referred to the decisions and interpretations of Largo Caballero.

The entire activity of the republican-socialist coalition in matters of labour policy consisted in the attempts fostered by the Government departments to secure for the U.G.T., a position of monopoly in labour matters, and to eliminate all other tendencies within the workers' movement. At the same time the real activities for labour reforms were pushed into the background. Neither the contemplated social insurance nor unemployment relief were introduced. The unemployed mounted to over a million. Begging and vagrancy increased tremendously; crime spread more and more.

A passing glance at the conflicts that rocked the Spanish Republic between 1931 and 1934 shows that the revolution of April 1931 was not completed, but went forward to bigger revolutionary outbursts. The social organism, having been shaken to its foundations, was unable to regain any stability.

When the Azana government resigned in the autumn of 1933, not less than 9,000 militants of the C.N.T., were in Spanish prisons. Up to that time 331 workers had been shot by the police since the proclamation of the Republic.

STRIKES AND STRUGGLES OF THE C.N.T. AND F.A.I.

One of the first large struggles waged by the workers under the republic was the strike of the telephone workers in 1931. The Government suppressed it brutally to eliminate any revolutionary activity which might be detrimental to the American-owned Telephone Company. The strike lasted for months. On July 8th 1931, the Chief of the State Police ordered all Civil Guards to lie in ambush on the highways and to shoot without warning anybody who was suspected of tampering with telegraph poles etc. The Minister of the Interior, Maura, had all strikers systematically arrested. They were later replaced by social-democratic union men.

In September 1931, the C.N.T., in Barcelona declared a General Strike as a protest against the mistreatment of political prisoners. The police stormed the local branches of the C.N.T., unions, but succeeded in occupying the building workers' union headquarters only after a lengthy siege.

During the summer of 1931 the agricultural labourers' strike in Andalucia took place; and the City of Seville declared a general strike in solidarity with the rural workers. The Civil Guard arrested four workers and shot them "while trying to escape." The General in command had the headquarters of the C.N.T., shot to pieces by the artillery.

In January 1932 the first social revolutionary uprising on a large scale took place. During a strike in Figols (Catalonia) the local miners started to take possession of the mines, to disarm the rich, and to proclaim libertarian communism. The movement extended into the entire region of the upper Llobregat river. Everything proceeded peacefully all in orderly fashion when the government ordered a large detachment of police to suppress the movement; after that, Anarchists were arrested en masse; 120 of them were exiled to Spanish Guinea, where they had to live under the most terrible conditions, which caused the death of one of them. The events, in their turn, led to a protest in the form of a General Strike, which extended to cities and to villages all over Spain. During this strike the police shot three children who were playing in front of a house in Navalmoral (Estremadura). In Tarrasa the Anarchists took possession of the City Hall, raised the red and black flag of the C.N.T., and proclaimed libertarian communism. The leaders of this uprising were condemned to twenty years' imprisonment.

One of the most magnificent strike movements started in the Autumn 1932 in the iron works of La Felguera (Asturias). There a number of aged workingmen had been dismissed and were not to get any old age pension. Then all the workers of the plant struck. This movement developed into a general strike in La Felguera and was followed by a general strike all over the Asturias. This example is typical of the Spanish class struggle. Actions of solidarity play the most important part. The proclamations of the strike committee of La Felguera show this characteristic strongly. One of them reads as follows:—

"The workers must not fail their brothers, grown old at the work bench, who have taught them their trade and given them a shining example of how to fight."

The ultimate goal of the movement: the social liberation of all, was the guiding spirit of every one of these struggles.

The Tragedy of 1933   The year of 1933 started with a new tragedy for the revolutionary movement.   In Barcelona an uprising of the Anarchist Federation of Iberia had broken out; it spread to villages and small towns in Valencia and Andalusia where the workers believed the hour of the final struggle had arrived.   In Casas Viejas (Cadiz) the workers also seized the village had tried to organise production and distribution on a communistic basis.   The government sent strong police detachments to the village.   Prime Minister Azana in person told police officers: "Neither wound, nor take prisoners who will only be found innocent later! Shoot them straight in the belly!"   The same instructions were given by the Minister of the Interior and the Head of the Police to the leader of the Guardia de Asalto who promptly carried out his duty.   Obviously these orders had been prompted by decisions of the entire Cabinet, probably with the sanction of the Socialist Ministers.   Thus in Casas Viejas, after the village had been conquered and many old and young men, women and children, had perished in a cabin that had been set on fire, twenty-three unarmed prisoners were shot by the police without any reason.   The police officer in charge was sentenced to thirty years in prison for having committed a sixteen-fold murder.   The responsible party in the Government escaped unscathed.

In the country, in the villages, every year, especially in Spring, revolutionary mass actions almost always started spontaneously, without being led by any organisation.   The workers ransacked olive storehouses and granaries; in many villages they drove the landowners out of their houses, and began to cultivate the unploughed fields for their own benefit until the Civil Guard stopped them.   Thousands of farm labourers were driven to such acts of despair by stark hunger.

Successful strikes   Strike movements in the rural districts also occured frequently.   Every one of these strikes was declared illegal by the Azana government.   In 1932, the Minister of the Interior said once that he would "place a policeman near each corn stalk" to safeguard the harvesting. That year the labourers actually worked under the bayonets of the Civil Guard.   In spite of that there were successful strikes in the rural districts, one of the most remarkable taking place in the environs of the famous wine city of Jerez in the Spring of 1933.   Here the workers in the vineyards walked out to improve their living and working conditions.   After the strike had lasted more than a month, the C.N.T., inspired all labour organisations in the city of Jerez to show their solidarity by a general strike.   This was carried out.   No newspaper appeared, no bread was baked, all cafes were closed in Jerez.   The vineyard workers won their point: their daily wages were raised to 9.75 pesetas, working hours were shortened to six hours and fifteen minutes, and one hour each for breakfast and lunch, and six recesses called "cigars", consisting of fifteen minutes each, were allowed.

Vegetable people   It would, of course, be utterly wrong to draw conclusions from the conditions of these workers and to apply them to Spanish farm labourers in general.   The great mass of the rural proletariat continued to live under absolutely inhuman conditions.   Even a bourgeois paper in Barcelona wrote about this topic in 1934:—

"Spain, so geography tells us, is a nation of twenty-two million people. But from an economic point of view, the country has only fourteen million inhabitants. There are actually existing in Spain eight million human beings that do not consume anything. They vegetate, but they do not live. What do these people purchase during the entire year? Well, these eight million of poor farm labourers and midget farmers, especially in Andalusia and Estremadura, buy themselves two pair of cloth shoes and one pair of very cheap trousers per annum. This enormous number of people does not mean anything to Spanish industry."

And this after three years of the Republic, of agrarian reform and socialist labour policy!

From among the tens of thousands of strikes that succeeded one another during recent years, we can record here only a few. Let us mention the national general strike, organised as a protest against the mass arrests and the closing of many trade unions, in the beginning of May 1933, which spread all over the country, wherever the C.N.T., had any influence. The Government was much concerned over the strike, the newspapers wrote of nothing else for days.

C.N.T. in the strikes   In the summer of 1933, a movement for shorter hours and corresponding increase of wages started in different parts of Spain. The building workers of Barcelona struck for this purpose for four months. Their demand for reduction of working hours was granted only in part, but their wages were increased, so that their earnings were not reduced. Activities of this kind started in several places in Catalonia and spread to the rest of Spain. Wherever the C.N.T., could influence the course of events, better wages were obtained, so that the decrease in working hours never meant a loss of wages. If the Spanish proletariat was generally able to keep its wages at the same level or could obtain better pay during the two and a half years after the proclamation of the Revolution, this was almost exclusively due to the numerous bitter fights led by the Confederation not only against the bosses, but also against the authorities which in every case sided with the capitalists. Every one of the big strikes of the C.N.T., was declared illegal, and always the armed forces were called out against the workers; clashes occurred regularly; streets were red with blood and prisoners were taken. Thousands of workers were kept in jail without knowing why.

Wages   It is hard to say anything about the wages of the workers in Spain. Daily wages in the larger cities ranged (during the Republic) from nine to fifteen pesetas, while they were much lower in the country. In the villages of the farm labourers, the daily earnings amounted to two pesetas or less, and the work was only seasonal. The trade unions of the C.N.T., tried as far as possible to carry into the collective agreements the principle of wage equalisation and to reduce the difference in wages among the many classes of workers. They succeeded in many cases in obtaining favourable regulations concerning holidays. The bosses were obliged to continue paying for several weeks a large percentage of workers' wages in case of illness. The syndicalist gas workers of Barcelona had a clause in their agreement to the effect that every worker who went to prison for political reasons had to be reinstated if his jail sentence did not exceed a certain number of years.

22

In connection with the union fights of the Spanish workers the two other great weapons of direct action must be mentioned: Sabotage and Boycott were liberally used. After a thoroughly organised three weeks' traffic strike in Barcelona, towards the end of 1933, the street car companies dismissed 400 syndicalist workers. This was met by an embittered sabotage campaign. Dozens of valuable street cars were destroyed by fire on remote lines. Finally all means of communication in Barcelona began to function again only under strong police guard. Numerous Spanish industries were successfully boycotted. The biggest action of this kind was against the Damm Brewery in Barcelona, which had dismissed around seventy workers of the C.N.T., after the General Strike in May 1933. The boycott slogan spread all over Spain, the firm sought to avoid the ruinous consequences by delivering their beer without a label. In many cafes where the boycotted beer was served, bombs exploded. Finally the concern gave in, put the dismissed workers back on the job, and paid a large compensation, most of which was used for the political prisoners.

JOINT ACTION GROWS DESPITE SOCIALIST PARTY BETRAYALS IN THE FIGHT AGAINST RIGHT ELECTION VICTORY

During the summer of 1933 the political situation in Spain came to a head, and severe conflicts were threatening. By-elections to various district bodies, municipal parliaments and elections of justices of the court of constitutional directors showed that the majority of the voters no longer sided with the Republican-Socialist soalition. Azana resigned, and Lerroux dissolved the constituent assembly.

This forced the workers to a decision. Were they again to take part in elections or should they draw their conclusions from the sharpening of social contradictions and start a revolutionary action? The C.N.T., unmistakably declared themselves for the latter, advocating abstention from voting and preparation for revolution.

The C.N.T., declared: the revolutionary worker cannot give his vote either to fascism and reaction or to the bourgeois parties of the Centre, but he has also been taught by the tragic breakdown of the German labour movement that a socialist-communist parliamentarism cannot check the catastrophe and is only able to create tragic illusions.

The socialist party wanted to have its cake and eat it. Largo Caballero, who in the meantime had become the guiding spirit of the radical wing of the Party, stressed in many speeches the uselessness of Parliamentary ballyhoo, but advocated participation in elections just the same. But, he maintained, if the reaction should win the elections, then the revolution should be started and civil war launched. The Socialist Party, Caballero declared, would never again enter into a coalition with the bourgeois parties, but from now on work only for the revolution inside and outside of the Parliament. This turn swung part of the socialist masses towards more radical methods, especially the youth who were ready to sacrifice their lives side by side with the revolutionary workers of the C.N.T., for the sake of final combat.

Elections of 1933 Elections took place; the revolutionary sections of the masses refrained from going to the polls and the Socialist Party lost half its seats. The Radical Party, of the great "man of affairs" and opportunist politician, Lerroux, obtained the biggest representation in the new Cortes, which was now dominated by a strong Right Wing.

The Socialist Party was rendered powerless in the parliament; the party of Lerroux reigned under the unconcealed dictatorship of the Right, which tolerated it for some time. The hour to deal a great blow against the system had come. The Socialists did not do anything. Not so the C.N.T. Believing firmly that the Socialist masses behind Caballero were ready to fight the last battle, the C.N.T., started a general uprising all over the country on the day the new Cortes was opened, December 8th 1933. The workers proclaimed a general strike and attacked the armed forces.

THE REVOLT OF 1933

In several districts the uprising was completely victorious. In many villages and small towns of Aragon, Rioja, Galicia and Catalonia, the workers disarmed the bourgeoisie, drove out or imprisoned the police, and proclaimed libertarian communism.

A manifesto of the revolutionary committee was distributed throughout the country declaring that the means of production were no longer private property, and asking the workers to take production into their own hands, to confiscate all stored provisions in villages and towns, and to reorganise the distribution of goods in the socialist manner by eliminating capitalist money. The labour organisations were to arm and not to allow any new power to dominate them, but to carry on alone the organisation of the new communistic life. The government immediately declared a "state of alarm" (which, in different forms, lasted until the next elections and was at one time extended into civil martial law). The workers of the C.N.T., soon saw clearly that the Socialist Party and the U.G.T., were sabotaging the uprising.

The realisation of this situation had a paralysing effect in some parts of the country, where as a result, the movement did not grow beyond a general strike, while in other regions the rebellious workers fought desperately to the last. In Hospitalet, a suburb of Barcelona, the fight lasted two weeks; Zaragoza, the capital of Aragon, was taken by the armed forces after a bitter struggle and so were likewise hundreds of revolutionary strongholds in the rural districts. Many armed revolutionaries fled into the hills; a great number perished through exposure and starvation in the snowed-in mountains.

The leadership of the radical wing of the Socialist Party kept aloof in the hope that after the destruction of the C.N.T., the Party would benefit by the growing revolutionary consciousness of the people. Through these tactics Largo Caballero believed the Socialists would be able to carry through their line of action. This attitude greatly embittered the revolutionary workers of the C.N.T. Suspicion against the Socialist leaders grew. These are the psychologic roots of the sad fact that in the course of 1934 no revolutionary unity could be attained between the workers of the U.G.T., and the C.N.T.

United Front   In spite of that, the discussion of a united front was taken up all over the country. Largo Caballero himself started it in several public speeches. The C.N.T., of the Central region published a manifesto which stated that the question of a united front had to be discussed in spite of the treason of the Socialist leaders.

It was of course, not so easy to find a common ground for an understanding. A united front meant to the Socialists simply that the anarchist workers should accept the party slogans. What did the Spanish Socialist Party want? According to a long speech by Prieto about that time in the Cortes, which held approximately the middle ground between the different tendencies within the party, the Socialist Party had the following principles:

Preserving the political and administrative government apparatus, a "cleansing" of the officials in favour of socialist office-hunters, preservation of the army, officers being appointed from the ranks; more liberal chances for advancement,

the owner of the soil to be the State, which should also determine the amount of rent,

gradual socialisation of industry which was to be managed ɩy persons belonging to the middle classes,

a fight against unemployment,

public works,

comprehensive elementary education.

It is possible that Largo Caballero's ideas went further than this, but in all his speeches he demanded solely that the party should seize power — and no one else but the party. Only then a policy of socialism could be undertaken. The concrete absorption of the anarchist workers were not granted the least concession, they were not mentioned a single time by the speakers of the radical wing of the party.

The programme of the C.N.T., was characterised by the following demands:

Complete expropriation of the bourgeoisie without any compensation,

abolition of the army,

arming of the workers,

organisation of the económic life and defence of the revolution by the trade unions and free revolutionary communes organised from below,

the decisive initiative always to rest with the workers and their own industrial and local organisations; the function and the jurisdiction of delegates of the district, regional and national organisations to decrease in reverse proportion to the scope of the body,

abolition of the Church,

communist or communal tilling of the soil,

firm establishment of the federalist principles in building up the socialist commonwealth.

These two programmes show the dominating tendencies in the Spanish labour movement prior to the Civil War. Other trends having followers among the workers only represented a minority. In 1934, the Communist Party had some influence in trade unions of the U.G.T., in Madrid, Toledo, Sevilla and the North, but it was unable to start any action independently of the U.G.T. In the 1933 Autumn elections it was successful in obtaining a number of votes, but it won only one seat in Malaga — the only Communist in the Cortes. In Barcelona, centre of Spanish industry, the Communist Party received only 1500 votes.

Besides the Communist Party, there was (especially in Catalonia) a strong independent Communist Party (the P.O.U.M. — workers' party of unified Marxists) opposing the official party line and approaching the left wing of the Socialist Party. Their leader, Maurin, obtained 1900 votes at the Cortes election in Barcelona. (It affiliated to the "Two-and-a-Half International" with the British Independent Labour Party, the Austrian Social Democrats, and others). There was also a Trotskyite faction.

The stronghold of the U.G.T., and the Socialists was in Madrid and in the North; the U.G.T., also had some influence among the agricultural workers in some districts of the South. There was also an Independent Socialist Party in Catalonia, differing from the official Party by reason of its Catalan nationalism. All the Marxists, including the communist factions, both Socialist parties, and the U.G.T., were unable to raise more than 40 000 votes in an industrial centre like Catalonia (with 2.5 million inhabitants).

Unfavourable Conditions for the C.N.T. The most significant labour groups in Spain remained the masses organised in the C.N.T., and the U.G.T. An extensive discussion developed between them in the beginning of 1934. It took place under conditions that were extremely unfavourable for the C.N.T. After the December uprising had been crushed, about 16,000 militants of the C.N.T., were sent to prison. The Confederation did not have a single paper, its entire press had been prohibited and its organisations had all been officially dissolved. The Socialist Party worked openly, and had at its disposal a daily paper in Madrid, while neither daily paper of the C.N.T., in Madrid nor in Barcelona appeared any more. Several militants of the C.N.T., made far-reaching proposals for a United Front. Others declined to confer with Socialist leaders, but gave assurances that, in case of emergency, they would co-operate with the workers of the U.G.T., without however, recognising their leaders. A well-known agitator of the C.N.T., made a concrete proposition for a united front in the Madrid daily "La Tierra": he had worked out a plan according to which the most important public services would be centralised. The formation of a centralistic bureaucracy would be prevented and the entire administration of economic life left to labour unions. He pleaded for a revolutionary workers' democracy where both mass organisations — U.G.T. and C.N.T. could exist side by side.

Neither the U.G.T., nor the Socialist Party ever responded to these proposals in public.

To clarify their inner situation, the C.N.T., held a secret conference of delegates from all regions in February 1934, where a definite stand on the united front question was taken. In a resolution which was published later, this conference asked the U.G.T., directly what were its revolutionary aims. The resolution declared further that the C.N.T., could not collaborate with political parties but was willing to come to an understanding with labour unions.

The C.N.T., never got a reply to this official resolution. It is easy to imagine the effect of this ambiguous attitude of the Socialist leaders had on the C.N.T., workers.

Other events in the course of the year helped to strengthen the doubts of the C.N.T., in the honesty of the leaders of the Socialist Party. When a conflict broke out between the "Left" government of the autonomous Catalan region and the central authorities of Madrid, the Socialist Party sided openly with the bourgeois-republican government of Catalonia and forgot its promise never to enter into a political bargain with the bourgeois parties.

But the S.P., went still further. There was likewise a conflict between the municipalities of the Basque provinces and the central government on matters of administration and State finances. The Basque Separatists availed themselves of this situation to stir up their regionalist movement. It should be noted that the Basque Separatist movement was clerical-traditionalist in character. The Socialists co-operated even with this movement. They signed an agreement saying that while the two parties were collaborating, the problem of social reform should not be touched!

When acting as chairman at a conference of Basque parli mentary representatives, the Socialist, Prieto, joined the delegates in singing loudly the Basque national anthem. This behaviour is the more remarkable if one considers the fact that, in spite of numerous opportunist breakdowns, the Spanish Socialists in all their history had consistently clung to at least *one* principle: the idea of centralism.

While the S.P. thus held several irons in the fire, it was at the same time preparing for revolutionary possibilities. It favoured the formation of so-called "Workers' Alliances" all over the country, embracing the Socialist Party, U.G.T., autonomous unions, the independent Communist parties and other small labour groups. These alliances looked upon themselves as storm troops of Largo Caballero. The C.N.T., did not join them. The official Communist Party only changed its negative attitude after the 1934 rebellion and became a member of the regional alliances. (There was still no centralised organisation). The alliance flourished above all in Catalonia, where the U.G.T., was scarcely represented, but where – outside the C.N.T., – there were strong "autonomous" and "non-political" unions that were practically at the disposal of Largo Caballero. The leftist government of Catalonia had prohibited the C.N.T., but favoured the Alliances lined up with the Catalan Government on October 5th 1934.

The situation in the Asturias was entirely different. This was the only region in Spain where the workers of the C.N.T., and U.G.T., overcame all differences and succeeded in forming a free alliance between their organisations.

THE ORIGIN OF THE ASTURIAS RISING

In doing this they thought more about the present combat than the future social structure; they gave no dogmatic directions to each other. In October all Asturias rose as one man. While the makeshift armoured cars of the workers in Oviedo (the capital of Asturias) bore the inscription "C.N.T.-F.A.I.", the Socialist workers in the villages fought under their banners for the mines. There were no actual differences between them as far as practical organisation of the fight and taking care of the needs of the population was concerned. The workers themselves had taken their fate in their own hands; they were on the road to direct understanding

After the unsuccessful rising of December 1933 the revolutionary spirit kept on growing. A judge in Zaragoza ordered the prohibition of the

C.N.T., but it continued to exist illegally. The April amnesty applied by the Lerroux Government was only for monarchists. Only part of the Anarchists were released. Over 8,000 of them had to remain in prison. In the same month of April the C.N.T., proved anew its unbroken revolutionary power by organising a few weeks' general strike in Zaragoza which totally paralysed the life of the city. The U.G.T., joined the C.N.T. Again the "united front from below" had taken place without negotiations or pacts. This giant strike, which caused keen excitement all over Spain. had no material aims, but was an act of solidarity for the sake of political prisoners and dismissed workers. At the same time the U.G.T., and C.N.T, in Madrid carried on a successful metal workers' strike for shorter hours and better wages, the autonomous trade unions in Valencia started a powerful general strike to aid the fighting workers of the electric power plants.

In all these fights the workers of the U.G.T., and other formerly inactive labour groups took a very energetic part. After the resignation of the Socialist Cabinet ministers, the leaders of the U.G.T., no longer kept its members from striking. This resulted in a completely different situation, but in spite of or perhaps on account of that, the confidence of the C.N.T. workers in the socialist leaders did not increase. The fighting spirit of the U.G.T., seemed to depend largely upon whether their leaders had cabinet posts in the Government. Once they had lost their soft jobs the former reformists seemed suddenly to turn into revolutionaries!

However, there was a genuine revolutionary change of heart as far as the larger part of the U.G.T., workers were concerned. Above all, the youth organisations and the Asturian workers made preparations for a revolution. They gathered arms etc., but they lacked a clear and uniform revolutionary plan of action. The conduct of the leaders in the Basque and Catalan conflicts may be interpreted in many ways.

This was the situation when the Cabinet change of October 4th 1934 took place. The Samper government had shown itself too "soft" during the conflict with the Catalan government. The reactionaries had expected an energetic shake-up in Catalonia. But Samper did not have enough courage for that. As a result, he lost the support of the Right and had to hand in his resignation on October 1st. The new Cabinet of Lerroux which consisted mostly of members of the Radical Party had for the first time, three Rightist ministers, henchmen of Gil Robles. He was the leader of the united reactionary forces, that is the Catholic Popular Action and the Agrarians. His programme was a Catholic fascism advocating the "corporate state" according to the pattern of Austrian cleric-fascism. The inclusion of these Catholic Monarchist Ministers in the Cabinet of a Republican Government was a danger signal to the workers. Spain seemed to have entered a situation similar to that of the Von Papen period in Germany which was a prelude to Hitler. Fascism already appeared at the gates.

THE OCTOBER REVOLUTION OF 1934
Curtain Raiser for 1936

At that moment the regional Workers' Alliances took the initiative and started a protest movement which found its expression in general strikes which spread all over Spain starting on October 5th. The C.N.T. took part in these protest strikes in several cities, such as Madrid, where the strike lasted nine days and led to numerous encounters. The C.N.T. stood at attention, ready as always to support the fight against fascism, but they did not want to be merely pawns in a strike movement which was essentially directed by the Socialist Alliances.

It was impossible for the C.N.T., to take part in the separatist movement which started at the same time in Catalonia. Here too the Workers' Alliance had proclaimed the general strike, but from the first day it was supported only by its own men in the various branches of the transport system, by the lower middle classes, and the commercial and office employees. The Catalan government supported the strike with all its strength. Under the very eyes of the police in Barcelona, the youth organisations of the Government party were armed, and the C.N.T., workers were chased out of their shops by force of arms so that, by October 6th, the strike was general.

On October 5th, right at the beginning of the strike, the Catalan Minister of the Interior had a large number of well-known anarchists imprisoned, lest the separatist movement, including the Workers' Alliance under the leadership of the ministers, be "disturbed". This situation caused the C.N.T., to publish a short manifesto, wherein they declared that they supported the protest against fascism, adding that they would not lend a hand to party politics or separatist tendencies. The Workers' Alliance in Catalonia was ready merely to support the radical wing of the Catalan governing party which urged the proclamation of an independent Catalan republic. During the morning of October 6th, the C.N.T., started to act on their own in several parts of Barcelona by re-opening their local branches and halls which had for ten months been closed by the police. But the police attacked the local branches again and the syndicalists had to withdraw.

Catalan Independence Fiasco In the evening of October 6th the Catalan Government hastened to proclaim the independent Catalan Republic a "member of a federal Spanish Republic," the Catalan government being provisionally in charge of its administration. This implied the repudiation of the Madrid government. But they failed to reckon with the Spanish government troops that were stationed in Barcelona who, instead of placing themselves at the disposal of the rebellious government, attacked it. The civilians that had been armed by the Catalan government, left their rifles in the street; the Catalan police surrendered the following morning, and the Catalan government capitulated, its power falling into the hands of the Spanish Army general in charge of the troops in Catalonia.

Church Burning In Asturias the movement developed in an entirely different direction, broadening into a social revolutionary uprising like nothing Spain had ever seen before. The alliance between C.N.T., and U.G.T., had borne fruit; the revolutionaries took possession of many towns and villages; the miners took over the mines. Revolutionary committees began to reorganise the distribution of food through coupons. Churches, government buildings were burned. In Bembibre, as in many other places, the workers spilled petroleum in the churches. But before lighting it, they took out the image of Christ and put it on the public square with the following inscription: "Red Christ! We respect you because you belong to us."

Fighting in Asturias   The Asturian revolutionaries had an advantage because they had plenty of arms. Part of these they had procured during the previous month, and in addition had seized, on the first day of the uprising, the big State ammunition factory at Trubia where not only rifles and ammunition but also brand new small canon and several tanks fell into their hands.

But the movement was cut off from the rest of Spain. The government did not allow any news to penetrate and was able to throw great masses of troops — African Foreign Legion and Arab regiments — into the Asturias. Thus it became master of the situation. The fighting was terrible. Thousands were killed. Among them was the leading C.N.T., militant in Asturia the anarcho-syndicalist, **Jose Maria Martinez**. Thousands of workers were imprisoned. The artillery of the government troops spread everywhere. (Later the press ascribed this destruction to the rebels). Large detachments of armed revolutionaries fled into the mountains, where the troops were unable to follow them.

FORWARD TO 1936!

It was one of the greatest tragedies of the Spanish revolution that the Asturias rebellion remained isolated and was defeated. There are a number of reasons for this: the socialist protest movement which started on October 5th had no uniform aim: in Catalonia it was made to serve merely the interests of a bourgeois-republican party.   On the other hand, the C.N.T., was likewise unable to control the situation and give a clear revolutionary aim to the confused mass action. But of course, as a glance at the history of Spain since 1934 shows, the resistance of the Spanish working class to fascism was not yet broken. After the defeat of the October 1934 Revolution, the entire Spanish workers' movement faced the position which the C.N.T., had to face practically all the time: its organisations were prohibited, its newspapers ceased to appear, its most active militants were arrested. As the Spanish revolutionary worker was accustomed to underground activities, however, this did not signify by any means that the organisations ceased to function or that their fighting spirit died down.

The political development of Spain very soon confronted the masses with the necessity of renewed action. Spain had come under the government of a parliamentary majority, but the composition of the Cabinet did not allow for a peaceful co-operation by the parties concerned within the parliamentary constitution for any length of time.

Moreover, another question was not settled; in what form was Catalan autonomy, as guaranteed by the constitution, to be restored? Certain political groups of the Catalan bourgeoisie demanded the preservation of autonomy, while the Spanish Rightist parties, headed by Gil Robles, wanted to put an end to it. At the bottom these differences could only be straightened out by a dictatorship. Meanwhile, in 1934, Spain had found itself in the grip of martial law, and the Government had allowed power to rest in the hands of the generals. They would not be easily satisfied to turn it over to a civilian government. Such a sharpening of the political had perforce to lead to a revival of the revolutionary movement. Spain would not lie down. It became the revolutionary storm centre of Europe.

Difficulties faced by the Spanish workers   The revolutionary workers had still to overcome great difficulties. Revolutionary unity of the workers had to come if capitalism were to be defeated. The united front of the revolutionary forces received its impetus from underground activities in prisons and dungeons. It was always, and remains, a special trait of the Spanish workers movement that its energies arehidden under the surface for a long time without seeming to break forth. All of a sudden the masses rise anew.   The Spanish revolutionary movement is not kept alive by theoretical insight or tactical plans – important as they may be – but rather by a dynamic revolutionary instinct, a mass passion which breaks out again and again and which cannot be conquered. It had some time to find its way to the road to social reconstruction. The constructive new organisation it was endeavouring to find would be something very different from what had been called socialism up to then, especially because of its libertarian character.

Socialism in Spain meant not only the striving for equality but above all, and constantly, the endeavour to create a life of freedom and self-determination, to found a new commonwealth which should be an alliance of independent individuals united of their own free will. It was inevitable that the Spanish revolution would discard various theoretical preconceptions of the anarchists as well as the socialists, but it had to have this particularly libertarian character which would be its special value for humanity.*

THE POPULAR FRONT   The governing party in Spain was the "Anti-Marxist Coalition", or C.E.D.A., and consisted on the Agrarian Party of Gil Robles (a landowners' and clerical party), the Navarre Nationalist Party (which unlike the Catalans and Basques was not separatist, but wished to see the successors of Don Carlos on the throne, rather than the successor, whoever it might be, of Alfonso XIII), and the Radical Party, whose leader, Lerroux was Prime Minister.

Because of the suppression of the October Revolt, the Workers' Alliance grew into a United Front of Socialists, separatists, and other independent parties.   Meanwhile, in the world outside, the menace of fascism was growing.   Moscow was already seeking to form a block of democratic powers against the Fascist powers, and to align itself with the former. It had given orders that United Fronts should be formed wherever possible, on an anti-fascist basis, and was prepared to broaden this to include capitalist and imperialist parties, provided only they were opposed to Hitler.   The Popular Front in France had already been formed – as an

*The original pamphlet by M. Dashar (only slightly amended in one or two phrases to bring it to date) concluded here, and was published in December 1934. The editor has ventured to continue the story to the outbreak of the Civil War.

31

alliance between Socialists and Communists. Moscow turned its attention to Spain. The heretofore small and neglected Communist Party was given aid, in order to build up a "Popular Front". From the first, therefore, it was in essence a Right-Wing Party, seeking only to unite "anti-Fascist" parties and not to push through a revolution. It was more "moderate" not in the sense that it was more averse to violence than anyone else, but that it wanted alliance with the bourgeoisie.

Throughout 1935 the air was tense, as the various forces began to do battle, often reaching armed conflict. There were never less than 30,000 political prisoners at any time. Widespread dissatisfaction with the economic position, disgust at the police brutality, and the example of Germany, led to a general working class feeling that the government had to be overthrown. By 1936 it could not resist the demand for elections. It went to the polls in February, and the Popular Front — despite a frenzied campaign by the Roman Catholic Church to stampede the faithful into voting for the Right — won an overwhelming victory, notwithstanding the control of the ballot-boxes by the Government. According to some "historians" the anarchists voted in this election. In fact the enormously increased vote for the Popular Front meant that if, in addition, the anarchists had abstained from voting as normal an overwhelming proportion of the electorate had rejected the Right Wing. Hence, all Right Wing commentators were convinced at the time that the anarchists had voted; Left Wing commentators were equally convinced they had not. In fact, while it cannot ever be proved whether all listened the C.N.T., did not advise its members to vote; it could hardly do so in view of its past experience of the politicians concerned. Many of its members did vote, nevertheless, hoping to get the political prisoners freed; many did not feel able to give up the principles of a lifetime. Had the C.N.T.-F.A.I., supported the Popular Front, the Right Wing would have had scarcely any seats in the Cortes. As it was, Azana formed the Popular Front Government, with a clear majority.

The Right-Wing now prepared for a coup d'etat; their ideal state was still Asturia, where fascism had shown itself capable of combining with Papal domination. It endeavoured to build a fascist movement, but lacked popular support such as characterised the German Nazis, and also lacked a leader of the calibre of Hitler or Mussolini. Nevertheless, the German example of Nazism was so vivid in Spain that even the Republican leaders recognised that it had to be fought against — especially they abhorred the persecution of Freemasons and the liberal academics; the fate of the Jewish professors and writers, friends of the Republican intelligentsia, showed them the dangers of fascism, though they still did not trust the people.

On the one hand the workers were demanding positive action. The peasants, refusing to submit to eternal poverty and premature death, were seizing landed estates. The workers in the towns, faced with paid strike-breakers and armed fascist vigilantes, fought it out both with the employer and on the streets.

The socialists in the government allowed the police to be used to suppress the working class and the peasants, but were less inclined to try to suppress the Right Wing extremists. However, with the examples of Germany and Italy before them, the workers were prepared to fight.

A few mild measures at land reform upset the aristocracy, but did not placate the workers. The Freemasons, who dominated the Liberal Republicans and middle-class Socialist lawyers, tried to curtail some of the privileges of the Church. It immediately entered the political battle with fierce determination to hold on to its privileges. One "reform" that outraged political Catholism was the fact that the Freemasons had legalised the small Protestant churches, a move typical of the government which wanted to give small reforms without undertaking major problems.

However, the libertarian workers still wanted to seize the Church lands, secularise the schools and hospitals, and abolish the confessional (which worked in co-operation with the police). They were not appeased by the legalised possibility of becoming Protestant which antagonised the Church at the same time.

In another bid to gain popularity, the Azana governme..t granted independence to the Basque, Catalan and Aragon provinces; but this measure of autonomy only won it the support of the Basque Catholics. The Catalan Nationalists were always suspect as to where their loyalties lay.

The Army While the C.N.T., called for the abolition of the Army, the Azana Government pursued the "realistic" line of "democratising" and "Catalanising" the Army. They knew that generals such as Mola, Queipo de Llano and Sanjurjo were arch-reactionaries and capable of plotting against the Government to which they had sworn allegiance. They therefore brought in Goded, to control the Army in Catalonia, and promoted Francisco Franco, who had been serving in Morocco. For some reason, they felt that such generals might prove "loyal."

Understanding that the military was plotting against it, the Government retired some generals and other officers were placed on pension. By doing so it had the officer class ranged against it. It sought to improve its relationship with France, and for this reason did not grant autonomy to Morocco. But Morocco remained firmly under the control of the military. It could not bring itself to the point of asking the Moors to turn upon the Army (this point of view, reinforced by the Communist Party in its 'Popular Front' period of advocating alliance with Britain and France against Germany, during which it abandoned the anti-imperialist struggle, remained a firm point of Republican policy and a condition of Communist support, throughout the Civil War).

The more military and Church plotted, and the more industrialists used armed force against the workers, the fiercer the libertarians fought back. They razed convents and monasteries and seized arms which were being stored for the coming right wing rebellion. (The English reader learned with shocked horror in his newspaper that the anarchists had burned down this or that convent or 'hospital' because "they had been refused arms" and wondered to what excess atheistic zeal could lead). Men who had for years been prominent in the struggle, such as Durruti and Ascaso, returned to Spain and joined in the new battle of the C.N.T.-F.A.I.

The Workers The workers would not stand idly by whilst the Army retained its power; and whilst the Right-Wing boasted of how it would seize power and create a corporate state. They were not going to be persecuted like the German workers; they shot down fascist leaders such as the young Primo de Rivera, son of the late dictator and founder of the

33

Falange. They seized arms where they could, often from churches where they were stored. They made plans to seize the estates which land reforms of the Government had promised them but which were still denied to them. The U.G.T., stood by the C.N.T., in many parts of Spain, notwithstanding the call of the Communist Party for an "anti-fascist front" that meant in effect, support for the bourgeoisie.

The right wing had various ideas about a coup. The monarchists plotted to restore the monarchy, but could not agree between Alfonsists and Carlists. The son of the former dictator Primo de Rivera, Jose Antonio Primo de Rivera (still remembered by Franquists as 'Jose Antonio') went to Mussolini's Italy to study the formation of a fascist party based on the exaltation of patriotism. The Falange which he founded in imitation of the Fascist movement, could not avoid imitating the C.N.T., which – though it despised patriotism as State subservience – was far more profoundly Spanish than any authoritarian movement could be.

Why Franco? Calvo Sotelo planned a union of the entire right wing which would stage-manage the coup which everybody now expected. He obtained the support of all sections of the monarchists, as well as of the Church and Falange, but he was shot. The Spanish workers did not want to see a Fuehrer. Jose Antonio was also shot. From then on, the military realised that it was impossible to recruit a Hitler or Mussolini from the civilian population. Only an Army general, secure among his troops, could govern Spain, and then only if he acted as if it were a conquered country. Even so, the leading generals were not safe. The wily, astute Francisco Franco was not originally the leader of the revolt. He got there, and stayed there, by intrigue, after the big men were killed. His family's Freemason connections, and his own Roman Catholicism, all helped him in his career first with the Republic, then with the stage managers of the coup. Juan March, the shady black-market millionaire from Majorca, was approached to finance the revolt. Franco represented himself to March as the go-between and to the Falange as one who admired Fascism and was willing to replace Jose Antonio. He gave contradictory promises to the Carlists and to the Alfonsists.

To foreign governments he gave the oily polished answers required of him.* He assured the English he would respect their commercial enterprises; he assured the French he would help them in Morocco; he told Hitler he was in favour of the great new Europe and assured the Vatican that his would be a "solution" similar to Mussolini's. Nobody expected any greater resistance than was usual to an Army takeover. The right wing had agreed to form an alternative government. The Azana government was ready to go through the liberal motions of protest and send protests to the League of Nations. But it did not seriously expect that there would be any resistance.

It knew there was no support among the people for Franco. The Falange in Barcelona contained a derisory 500, little more than the Communist Party (which was however growing in strength elsewhere in Spain, at the expense of the Socialist Party). It felt therefore that the rebels had no legal or moral rights. Some of its members were profoundly

---

*This experience stood him in great stead in World War II when he managed, despite his obligations to Hitler to avoid the slightest rupture with Great Britain.

shaken by events in Germany and Austria where "leading intellectuals" had been shot or humiliated and imprisoned, and respectable bourgeois liberals and social-democrats had found themselves outlawed. Because of this they were quite genuine in appealing to the workers' organisations "to be loyal to the republic" and to "stand by the legitimate government" though at a later period a great many of the republican-socialist middle class took steps to extricate themselves from the struggle unless, like Azana or Negrin, they were too deeply compromised.

Therefore, completely different pictures of Spain were presented to the world. Some, on the Right Wing, saw the scene as a crusade to save Spain from "communism and anarchy" — especially in the Roman Catholic world. Others saw a democratic Republic, threatened by the world sweep of Fascism.

So far as the great mass of the Spanish workers were concerned, it was the signal for Revolution and while they were quite content to let the politicians talk about the democratic republic for the benefit of the outside world, they themselves had no illusions. They answered military rebellion with the greatest force at their disposal: social expropriation. Faced with the irresistible drive for a social revolution; fearing lest social expropriation be made a fact; the leading capitalists conferred. Under the direction of multi-millionaire Juan March, and with the assistance of the Church, they formed a united front of Right Wing parties (other than separatist Catalans and Basques), and sought aid in Germany and Italy.

THE CIVIL WAR BEGINS It should have been a traditional coup d'etat. But the workers responded by a general strike and a counter-uprising. The C.N.T. and U.G.T., declared a general strike and armed resistance against the military rebellion. Everywhere workers, members of the C.N.T. or the U.G.T., rushed to the military barracks and overwhelmed the troops. The conscripts came over to the workers arms in hand. The Navy overthrew its officers and came to the support of the republic. The men and women in the towns seized old muskets from the Carlist war, butchers' knives, axes, anything that would serve as a weapon, and fell upon the militia. Within a few days, the rebellion was crushed, so far as Spain was concerned. Except where the military garrison had bolted itself in and was withstanding seige, and in a few strongholds such as Carlist Navarre, the right wing was in retreat. Leading members fled the country. Churches which had been used as arsenals went up in flames.

The army in Morocco acted decisively. It could not rely upon the fleet, but with the help of foreign ships and planes it crossed into Spain. The regular army, and the Moorish legions, marched in against the Spanish people, with considerable reinforcements from Italy. Aeroplane cover and support came from Germany and Italy. Step by step the remorseless military machine rolled into southern Spain. Where there was determined resistance, as in Malaga, and then in Seville, it was halted. But sheer military superiority won. And wherever the army moved in, there was a massacre. Not since the Moorish invasions had there been such determined fighting followed by massacre of the population. This was what the "patriotic exaltation" of the right wing had finally led to. With the workers using the strongest weapon in their armoury — social expropriation — the Right Wing had retaliated with the strongest weapon in its armoury — genocide.

Franco had landed in Morocco on July 17th; his rising began on the 18th; and on July 19th there was a social revolution throughout Spain. Taking heart at this response by barefisted workers against armed troops, the Government called upon them to resist. It declared itself the legal government and the army as mere rebels. But the impetus had gone far beyond anything the legal government could control. In Catalonia the banners of the C.N.T., and F.A.I., were everywhere. It was a veritable anarchist revolution. Elsewhere the flags of the C.N.T., and U.G.T., were intertwined. A new set on initials arose "U.H.P." — United Proletarian Brothers — and that signified unity between the C.N.T., and U.G.T. Everywhere the workers seized the factories, the peasants seized the land; the military were overwhelmed and their rifles taken from them and used against t' e next garrison. Churches, hastily requisitioned as garrisons by the Right Wing, went up in flames. Every species of weapon was dragged out; even museums were ransacked for muskets that had done duty in the Peninsular War. Scythes and kitchen knives were used in the battles for Barcelona, Seville, Valencia. Only the garrison towns of Burgos and Saragossa were held by the fascists. Faced with this situation, General Franco decided to invade Spain with Moroccan troops, mercenaries, and substantial aid from Germany and Italy. The Civil War had begun.

Behind the Republican lines, there also began the work of social expropriation. This was that socialism of a libertarian nature, with its special value for humanity, which was the result of years of work and struggle by the C.N.T.-F.A.I., of the temperament of the Spanish workers and of the universal yearning for freedom with dignity. Whatever political compromises might be followed, and whatever political and military defeats there were in store, SPAIN pointed the way to a new society.

A.M.

The Spanish Workers Movement

Albert Meltzer

This article first appeared in **Anarchy**, *No. 12 (2nd series) under the title* **The Labour Movement in Spain.**

On the whole there has been little or no study of the Spanish labour movement. The success of the insurrection against Tsarism so captivated the imagination of the world that attention, from the point of view of revolutionary socialism, has thereafter been riveted on Russia and what concerns its interests. The State "Socialism" that triumphed in that country is no doubt worth studying, if not experiencing: but from the standpoint of any sincere revolutionary — even one who might not consider himself a libertarian — it is surely more richly rewarding to look at the case of a labour movement that could sustain itself through generations of suppression; that could dispense with a bureaucracy; and that could maintain its character of control by the rank and file.

There are of course, faults and failures. These may be better understood following a study of the working class movement, and dispensing with the criticism of the anarcho-syndicalist offered by Trotskyist sources which make false comparisons out of context with Russia and deal with a period of only three years out of ninety; as a result of which, even among would-be libertarians, the years of struggle and achievements are dismissed with a vague reference to "bureaucracy" which asserted itself at that period, or among Marxists, with a titter — "he-he anarchists entered the Popular Front Government" — as if there was no more to be said on the matter.

The Spanish labour movement had five overlapping phases which can be summed up in five key words — the "international"; the "union"; the "revolution"; "anti-fascism"; and the "resistance". Each represents a different phase and the mistakes, and betrayals appear almost entirely in the fourth ("anti-fascist") phase.

The significant character of the movement is played down deliberately for a simple reason: it overwhelmingly disproves the Leninist thesis, equally flattering to the bourgeois academic, that the working-class, of itself, can only achieve a trade union consciousness — with the corollary that trade union consciousness must be confined to higher wages and better conditions, and without the guiding hand of the middle-class elitist, would never understand that it could change society.

The "International" Phase

The historians want on the one hand to say that Bakunin was a poseur who boasted of mythical secret societies that did not exist; and on the other hand that he, by sending an emissary (who did not speak Spanish) introduced anarchism into Spain. In fact, ever since the Napoleonic wars — and in some parts of Spain long before — the workers and peasants had been forming themselves into societies, which were secret out of grim necessity.

It is sometimes alleged that "liberal" ideas entered Spain only with the French invasion. What in fact came in — with freemasonry — was the political association of the middle class for liberal ideas (and the advancement of capitalism) against the upper classes, and their endeavour to use the working class in that struggle. But the working class and peasants had a known record of 400 years insurrection against the State. It is their risings and struggles, and the means employed — long before anarchism as such was introduced — that are used by historians as if they were describing Spanish anarchism. In Andalusia in particular the peasants refused to lie down and starve, or to emigrate en masse (only now is this political solution being forced on them); they endeavoured to make their oppressors emigrate — that is to say, to cause a revolution, even locally.

In the eighteen-thirties the co-operative idea was introduced to Spain (relying on early English experience); and the first ideas of socialism were discussed, basing themselves on the experiences of the Spanish workers and also borrowing from Fourier and Proudhon. The early workers' newspapers came out, especially in the fifties, and revealed the existence of workers' guilds in many industries, including the Workers' Mutual Aid Association. Because of the Carlist wars — and the periodic need to reconcile all "liberal" elements — a great deal of this went on publicly, some of it surreptitiously.

The first workers' school was founded in Madrid by Antonio Ignacio Cervera (fifty years before the more famous Modern School of Francisco Ferrer). He also founded a printing press whose periodicals reached workers all over the country. Cervera was repeatedly persecuted and imprisoned (he died in 1860). It was from the ideas of free association, municipal autonomy, workers' control and peasants' collectives that Francisco Pi y Margall, the philosopher, formulated his federalist ideas. The latter is regarded as "the father of anarchism" in Spain. But he did no more than give expression to ideas current for a long time.

During the period of the general strike in Barcelona (1855) the federations entered into relationship with the International Association of Workers in London (later called "The First International")' It was quickly realised that the ideas of the Spanish section of the International were far more in accord with Bakunin's Alliance than with the Marxists. In 1868 Guiseppe Fanelli was sent by Bakunin to contact the Internationalists in Spain. To his surprise — he barely spoke Spanish and said "I am no orator" — at his first meeting he captured the sympathy of all. Among his first "converts" the majority belonged to the printing trade — typographers like Anselmo Lorenzo, lithographers like Donadeu, engravers like Simancas and Velasco, bookbinders and others. It was they who were in Spain the most active, and the most literate of workers. They formed

38

the nucleus of the International. (Marx wrote gloomily to Engels: "We shall have to leave Spain to him [Bakunin] for the time being." 'By the time of the Congress in Barcelona in 1870, there were workers' federations throughout the country. The programme on which they stood: for local resistance, for municipal autonomy, for workers' control, for the seizure of the land by the peasants, has not since been bettered. They did not fail because they were wrong; merely because (like the Chartists in England) they were before their time. There was no viable economy to seize. They could do nothing but rise and fight.

The bourgeoisie had totally failed, during their long struggle with reaction, to modernise the country. The Government persistently retained control by the use of the army and of the system of Guardia Civil which it had copied from France.

Workers' Federations

In 1871 workers' federations existed in Madrid, Barcelona, Valencia Cartagena, Malaga, Cadiz, Libares, Alella, Bilbao, Santander, Igualada, Sevilla, Palma de Mallorca – taking no orders from a central leadership, standing on the basis of the local commune as the united expression of the workers' industrial federations, and in complete hostility to the ruling class. It was essentially a movement of craftsmen – as in England the skilled worker became a Radical, in Spain he became an Internationalist. Pride in craft became synonymous with independence of spirit. Just as in England, where the village blacksmith and shoemaker became the "village radical" who because of his independence from "the gentry" could express his own views, and become a focus for the agricultural workers' struggles – so in Spain he became an Internationalist (a stand which he easily combined with regionalism).

The first specifically anarchist nucleus began in Andalucia in 1869 – due to the work of Fermin Salvochea. It was there, too, that the International became strongest. As the repression grew so the anarchist ideas captured the whole of the working class movement. But the reason was not because Bakunin, Fanelli, Lorenzo or Salvochea had decided to give Spanish federalism a name, or to label it in a sectarian fashion. It was because the Marxist part of the International was growing away from them. During Marx's struggle with Bakunin he was forced more clearly to state his views in a specifically authoritarian manner. The idea of central State authority was precisely what repelled the Spanish Internationalists. The notion that they required a leadership from the centre was something they had already, in their own organisation, dispelled.

The International reached its peak during 1873/4. Its seizure of Cartagena – the Commune of Cartagena would take precedence over the Commune of Paris for the "storming of the heavens" if greater attention had been paid to it by historians outside Spain.

The Commune of Paris showed how the State could be instantly dispensed with; but its social programme was that of municipal ownership and it was in this sense that its adherents understood the word "communist". In Cartagena the idea of workers' councils was introduced – it was understood that what concerned the community should be dealt with by a federal union of these councils; but that the places of work should be controlled directly by those who worked in them. This "collectivism"

39

preceded by forty or fifty years the "soviets" of Russia (1905 and 1917) or the movements for workers' councils in Germany (1918) and profoundly affected the whole labour movement, which for the next twenty years was in underground war with the regime: bitterly repressed, and fighting back with guerrilla intensity.

The conceptions which the British shop stewards brought to bear on British industry – of horizontal control – during the First World War, of horizontal control to circumvent the trade union bureaucracy – were inbuilt into the Spanish workers' movement from the beginning. When the workers' federations turned from the idea of spontaneous insurrections to that of a revolutionary labour movement and began to form the trade union movement, it had already accepted the criticisms of bureaucracy which were not even made in other countries until some forty or fifty years of experience was to pass; it saw in a union bureaucracy the germs of a workers' state, which it in no way was prepared to accept. Moreover, the idea of socialist or liberal direction – urged by the freemasons – was seen quite clearly in its class context. It was this experience brought from the "International" period that made the labour movement the most revolutionary and libertarian that existed.

Regionalism

The essential regionalism of the Internationalist movement was somewhat different from trade unionism as it was understood in England. Instead of a national union of persons in the same craft, the basis of craft unionism, there was a regional federation of all workers. The federation divided into sections according to function. Thus it was possible for even individual craftsmen to be associated with the union movement, which accorded with the hatred most of the workers had for the factory system anyway. It also meant that when anyone was blacklisted for strike activities, he could always be set up on his own. Pride in craft was something ingrained in the internationalists. The most frequent form of sabotage against the employer was the "good work" strike – in which better work than he allows for is put into a job. It was something they employed even when there was no specific dispute (it is the reason why there were fewer State inspections of jobs for safety reasons and why today – the union movement having been smashed – one reads so frequently of dams breaking, hotels falling down or not completed to time, and so on). For this reason people trusted the union label when it was ultimately introduced and – despite the law and his own prejudices – an employer had to go to the revolutionaries to get the good workmen, or let the public know he was employing shoddy labour. "You are the robber, not us," was the statement most often hurled at the employer who wanted honesty checks on his workers.

"Regionalism" – the association of workers on the basis of locality first, and then into unions associated with the place of work – was something that concurred fully with the insurrectional character of the movement. Time and again a district rose and proclaimed "libertarian communism" rather than be starved to death or emigrate (the latter was years later, forced on them only by military conquest). It was for this reason that the seemingly pedantic debate began between "collectivism" or "communism" in the anarchist movement – fundamentally a

40

question as to whether the wage system be retained or not in a free society — since this was indeed an immediate issue in the collectivities and co-operatives established with a frequency as much as in modern Israel — though with the significant difference that it was in a war against the State and not with its tolerant assistance.

Formation of the C.N.T.

The workers' organisations persistently refused to enter into political activity of a parliamentary nature. It was the despair of the Republican and Socialist politicians, who were sure they could "direct" the movement into orthodox, legal channels. It was an attempt to divide the movement, not to unite it, that led to the formation of the Union General de Trabajadores (U.G.T.) in 1888. It was a dual union, with only 29 sections and some three thousand members. The congresses of the regional movement — the Internationalist movement which by now was transforming itself into an anarchist one — had seldom less than two or three hundred sections.

In the years of terror and counter-terror that followed, attacks on the workers' movement led to the recurrent individual counter-attacks of the 1900s, resulting in the enormous protests against the Moroccan War that culminated in the "Red Week" of Barcelona. Meantime the socialist movement stood aloof, trying to ingratiate itself with the authorities in the manner of the Labour movement in England — then still part of the Liberal Party. This demand for national-based craft unions (raised by the U.G.T.) thus became indentified with the desire for parliamentary representation in Madrid.

The Spanish movement was entering its "union" phase, influenced strongly by the syndicalism of France. The Solidaridad Obrera movement (Workers Solidarity) adopted the anti-parliamentary views of the French C.G.T. whose platform for direct workers' control was far in advance of the epoch, and which was already preparing the way for workers to take over their places of work, even introducing practical courses on workers' control to supplant capitalism.

As the anarcho-syndicalist movement developed in Spain after experience of the way in which the parliamentary socialists had gained creeping control of the syndicalist movement in France and debilitated this movement, it was inbuilt into the formation of the C.N.T. (Confederacion Nacional del Trabajo — National Confederation of Labour) that the movement should follow the traditions of federalism and regionalism that prevented the delegation of powers to a leadership. The C.N.T., was created in 1911 (at the famous conference at the salon de Bellas Artes in Barcelona) as the result of a demand to unite the various workers' federations all over the country — following strikes in Madrid, Bilbao, Sevilla, Jerez de la Frontera, Soria, Malaga, Tarrasa, Saragossa. It helped to organise a general strike the same year (as a result of which it became illegal).

It rose to overwhelming strength during the world war — its most famous test being the general strike arising from the strike at "La Canadiense." From then on, for 25 years, it was in constant battle, yet the State was never able to completely suppress it.

41

25 Years of Unionism

The complete failure of some libertarians to understand even the elementary principles of the C.N.T., throughout those years is staggering. When the structure and rules of the C.N.T., were reprinted in *Black Flag* some comments both privately and publicly left one amazed. One reader thought it was a "democratic centralist" body, when the whole shape and structure of it was obviously regionalist. For years, indeed, a major debate raged as to whether unions should be federated on a national basis at all. Some could not understand it *was* a union movement, and pointed out the lack of decisiveness in dealing with national (political) problems.

Another saw in the rule that delegates should not be criticised in public a libertarian version of "don't rock the boat, comrades"   comparing it with the determination of the T.U.C., not to let its leaders (quite a different matter) be criticised. But the delegates were elected for one year only. They could be recalled at a moment's notice if they were not representing the views of their members. Most of the time, as negotiating body, they were illegal or semi-legal. It was not pleasant for someone who avoided acting as a delegate, and who had the power to recall the delegate if there were sufficient members in agreement, to attack a named delegate in public. That is not the same thing at all as criticising a permanent leader or democratically-elected dictator such as one finds in British trade unionism. Nor is it the same thing as saying one should never criticise anyone at all. (It must, however, be held against the rule that in 1936/9 and after many refrained from criticising self-appointed spokesmen because of tradition).

Yet others, bringing a forced criticism of Spanish labour organisation in order to fit preconceived theories, have suggested it was subordinated to a political leadership, the Anarchist Federation playing a "Bolshevik" role (something quite inconceivable) or that of a Labour Party. What such critics cannot understand is that the anarchists relinquished the building of a political party of their own, and that it was only because of this that they had their special relationship with the C.N.T. Had they endeavoured to give it a political leadership, they would have succeeded in alienating themselves as did the Marxists. (The original Marxist party, the P.O.U.M., endeavoured for years to obtain control of the C.N.T: later when the Communist Party was introduced into Spain in the 'thirties, the P.O.U.M., was denounced as "trotskyist" and even "trotsky-fascist" by the Stalinists. The Trotskyists proper took the line that the very existence of a revolutionary union was an anachronism and they criticised the P.O.U.M., for trying to infiltrate the C.N.T., rather than to enter, and aspire to lead, the U.G.T., – though the latter was a minority organisation).

Like many other anarchist groups in other countries, those in Spain were based on affinity, or friendship, groups – which are both the most difficult for the police to penetrate, and give the most productive of results as against which is the positive danger of clique-ism, a problem never quite solved anywhere. The anarchists who became well known to the general public were those associated with exploits which no organisation could ever officially sanction. For instance, Buenaventura Durruti came to fame as the result of his shooting Archbishop Soldevila, in his own cathedral – in response to the murder, by gunmen of Soldevila's "Catholic" company union, of the general secretary of the C.N.T., the greatly loved Salvador Segui. With bank robberies to help strike funds, the names of the inseparable Durruti, Ascaso and Jover became household words to the many workers who faced privation and humiliation in their everyday life, and felt somehow revindicated as well as reinvigorated.

One must bear in mind the capitalist class was at this time engaged in its own struggle against the feudal elements in Spain (which even resisted the introduction of telephones). The economic struggle of capitalism (palely reflected in the political mirror as that of republicanism versus the monarchy) was an extremely difficult one: it made the struggle of the workers to survive that much more difficult. The employers did not have as much to yield as in other countries where industrialisation had progressed; had they in fact been further advanced, the amount so r ilitant an organisation could have obtained from capitalism would have been staggering.

As it was, capitalism fought a constant last-ditch stand against labour. It was a bloody one, too, and it should not be supposed that individual "terror" was on one side. The lawyer for the C.N.T., a paraplegic, well-known for his stand on civil liberties — Francisco Layret who could be compared with Benedict Birnberg here, who has complained that he has been put on a police black-list — was shot down in his wheelchair by employer's pistoleros.

It was against such pistoleros that the F.A.I., hit back. Anarchist assassination is taken out of its class context by Marxist critics. They did not think that individual attacks would "change society", that the capitalist class would be terrorised or the State converted by them. They hit back because those who do not do so, perish.

Unity

While the local federations always opposed any form of common action with the republican or local nationalist parties, and sometimes lumped (correctly) the Socialist Party with the bourgeois parties, nevertheless on the whole they deplored the division in the ranks of the proletariat and as the struggle deepened in the thirties could not see why they should be separated from the U.G.T., or the Marxist parties – the C.P., P.O.U.M., or some sections of the Socialist Party. "Unity" is always something that sounds attractive. But notwithstanding the adage it does not always mean strength. Those who desire it the most are those who must compromise the most and therefore become weak and vacillating.

The popular mistake, too, is to assume that because these parties were more "moderate" in their policies – that is to say, more favourably inclined to capitalism and less willing to change the economic basis of society – they were somehow more gentle in their approach, or pacific in their intentions. Under the Republic the "moderate" parties (which had collaborated with the dictatorship of Primo de Rivera under the monarchy) created the Assault Guards especially to hit the workers, and the C.N.T., in particular. To imagine an equivalent one must assume that in addition to the police, the Army are also on street patrol – as an equivalent to the Guardia Civil – but the Government brings in a special armed force (like the "B" Specials) to attack the T.U.C. This was a "moderate" policy as against the "extremism" of the anarchist who wanted to abolish the armed forces (which incidentally were plotting against the Republic). That was an "impractical and utopian" idea, said the Republicans and Socialists, who aimed to democratise the armed forces instead by purging it of older monarchists and bringing in young generals like Francisco Franco (whose brother was a Freemason and Republican, as well as a "national hero"), whose "loyalty" to the republic would be assured.

Problems

The problem that we are familiar with is that of a labour movement hesitant to take its opportunities, while the capitalist class seizes every possibility of advancing its interests. The problem for Spanish labour was different; namely, that while it was determined and even impatient for Revolution, the capitalist class remained (until only a comparatively few years ago, afraid to interfere politically lest it upset the equilibrium by which the military were the last resort of the regime, and unwilling to move too far ahead industrially for fear of the State power dominated by feudal reaction. Only a few foreign capitalists were willing to take the plunge in exploiting the country. Thus strike after strike developed into a general strike, and the confrontation thus achieved became a local insurrection, for the capitalists were asked more than they would or sometimes could grant.

It is the insurrections which have been more often the concern of the historians who inevitably talk of "the anarchists" and their conduct in running this or that local conflict: in reality, the anarchists had helped to create an organisation by which the workers and peasants could run such insurrections themselves. It is inevitable that because of this, mistakes of generalship would occur and it would be futile to deny that a highly organised political party could possibly have marshaled such forces much differently (this was the constant despair of the Marxist parties); but towards what end? The conquest of power by themselves. In rejecting this solution, other problems arose which must be the continued concern of revolutionaries.

What, after all, is the point of accepting a political leadership which seizes power — with no real benefit to the working class, as was the real case in Soviet Russia — by virtue of its brilliant leadership (and its tactical and tacit arrangements with imperialist powers) — or might (as the Communist Party did in Chiang's China or Weimar Germany) lead, with all its trained "cadres", to the same sort of defeat the man on the ground could quite easily manage for himself?

One other point must be taken into consideration, and that was the demoralisation of many militants after years of struggle in which enormous demands were made upon the delegates with absolutely no return whatever outside that received by all. There was no problem of bureaucracy (the general secretary was a paid official; beyond him there were never more than two or three paid officials) but than as a result there was no reward for the delegates, who suffered imprisonment — and the threat of death — and who needed to be of high moral integrity to undertake jobs involving negotiation, and even policy decisions of international consequence, that in other countries would lead to high office but in Spain led merely to a return to the work bench at best, or to jail and the firing squad at worst.

44

It is not a coincidence, nor the result of conscious "treachery", that many militants who came up through the syndicates* later discovered "reasons" for political collaboration or entry into the political parties, which alone offered rewards, and every one of which hankered after the libertarian union, which alone had a broad base that would mean certain victory for whoever could command it.

The student-movement-inspired thesis is wong: the F.A.I. was not a Bolshevik nor a social-democratic party. If it had been, this problem would not have arisen. The problems of Spanish labour in those years were not problems of political control, nor whether the tactics of this party or that party were right or wrong (that is to think of Spain in terms appropriate to the Stalin-Trotsky quarrel, but the dispute between the rival gangsters of the Kremlin is not necessarily applicable in every country). Basically they were the problems of freedom, and of mass participation in its own destiny. We must not delude ourselves that these do not exist.

With this background of the labour movement it was impossible for the capitalist class to switch it round on the basis of nationalism and harness it behind themselves, as they had done with temporary success in many countries in the First World War, and with some permanent (as it then seemed) success in the Nazi era. The Falange tried to ape the workers' syndicates but nobody was fooled who did not want to be. When the Falange failed in its task, as every attempt of the Spanish bourgeoisie failed — whether liberal, republican or fascist — the Army was brought in, in the classical manner of a ruling class holding power by force.

What took the ruling class by surprise — having seen the way in which the labour movements of the world caved in at the first blast of the trumpet (above all, the fabulous Red Army trained movement of the German workers under Marxist leadership reduced with one blow of the fist to a few, frightened people being beaten up in a warehouse) — was the resistance to the nation's own army by the working people. If at that moment the Popular Front (claiming to be against fascism) — realising its fate would be sealed with the victory of the Army — had armed the people the rising would have been over. The result of their refusing to do so meant that trench warfare could develop, in which (against heavy arms, and later troops and planes, coming in from the fascist countries) the Spaniards could only resist, keep on the defence, and never mount an attack; hence they would be bound to loose in the finish.

One of the most significant trends shown in July 1936 was the seizure of the factories and the land by the workers. This was an experience in workers' self-management which was not however unique — since the same attempts had been made by many collectives and co-operatives before — but whose scale was staggering — and which represented in itself a defiant gesture of resistance by the workers which the Popular Front Government wished to play down, and eventually suppress.

For this reason, the Popular Front has never since ceased, through its supporters at the time, to harp on one theme only: the International Brigade. But this merits a separate article.

*Pestana, for instance, once General Secretary, later hived off to form his own political party (the "Treintistas" — after his "Committee of Thirty.")

It was not merely the disciplinary and murderous drives by the Communist Party that destroyed the collectivisation and self-management. One must add to it the fact that as the civil war proceeded, the workers were leaving the factories in ever increasing numbers, for the front lines, which became even more restricted.

Divisions

The fact that the workers had, with practically their bare hands, prevented an immediate military victory and, as it seemed, prevented the rise of world fascism, caused a euphoric condition. The slogan was "United Proletarian Brothers": the flags of the C.N.T., mixed with those of the U.G.T. The Communists and Socialists were welcomed as fellow-workers, even the Republicans accepted for their sake. Undoubtedly the whole mass of C.N.T. workers — and others — welcomed this end of divisions which seemed pointless as against world fascism. In time of war one looks favourably upon any allies: no leadership could have prevailed against the feeling that there were no more divisions in the workers' ranks. On the contrary, those who now aspired to leadership — since the conditions of war were such that leadership could exist — began to extol the merits of their new-found allies.

Those who refer to the "atrocities" of the early period of the Civil War seldom point to the root cause of many of them: the fact that the Republican authority was now officially on the side of the workers. A simple illustration was told me by Miguel Garcia of how, in the early days in Barcelona the group he was with seizing arms from the gunsmiths' to fight the army, came in confrontation with a troop of armed Guardia Civil, the hated enemy. The officer in charge signalled them to pass. They did so silently, waiting to dash for it — expecting to be shot in the back in accordance with the *ley de fuga*. But the officer saluted. The Guardia Civil was loyal to the Government. In many villages the people stormed the police barracks demanding vengeance on the enemy. They were greeted with cries of "Viva la Republica." We are your allies now. We are the officers of the Popular Front. Ask your allies in the Republican and Socialist parties if it is not so."

Even so, many anarchists never trusted them.

It was the police and Guardia Civil who were the most vicious to the fascists whom they had to detain, to show their enthusiasm for the popular cause. Later, when the tides of war had changed, they had to be even more vicious to the anti-fascists, to show that they had never ceased in allegiance to the properly constituted authority.

The Compromises

It is relevant to this description of the Spanish labour movement to trace the dissolution of the C.N.T., since with the drift from the factories it ceased to be a union movement and became, in effect, as association of militants.

During the war what was in effect a demoralisation of many militants set in, and a division occurred between "well-known names" and those who really made up the organised movement (the rank and file militants, *militantes de base*,) since the demand for unity, understandable as it was,

46

led to a collaboration with the republican government under the slogan of "U.H.P." All those who had for years been denied a recognition of their talents — and craved for it — now had their chance. Majors, generals; in the police and in the direction of government; even in the ministries themselves. Those who so collaborated did not really go as representatives either of the anarchist movement or of the labour organisation although their collaboration was passively accepted by most. They took advantage of the greatest weakness of the traditional anarchist movement, the "personality cult" (as witness Kropotkin, individually supporting World War I, and causing enormous damage to the movement which he in no way represented and from which his "credentials" could not be withdrawn for there were none except moral recognition).

The emergence of an orator like Garcia Oliver, or Federica Montseny, as a Minister purporting to represent the C.N.T., was a symptom of these collaborationist moves. Keeping the matter in proportion their betrayals and compromises were effected by the defeat, and were not its cause.

It was, however, this division that disorientated the organisation in subsequent years.

Following the defeat, the libertarian movement was re-established in a General Council in Paris in February 1939. The existing secretary of the C.N.T., Mariano Vasquez, was appointed secretary of the Council. But this was in no way a trades union. It was a council of war, intending to maintain contact between the exiles now scattered round the world, and in particular those in France, where the majority were in concentration camps, set up with barbed wire and guarded by Senegalese soldiers, as if they were P.O.W.s, but under conditions forbidden by the Geneva Convention.

There were no longer meetings appointing delegates subject to recall, nor any check upon the representatives of the movement. Nobody in any case was interested. The working class of Spain had been decisively smashed. Its organisations were in ruins. Those in exile had to build a new life. Those inside Spain were facing daily denunciations leading to the firing squad and prison. The children of the executed and imprisoned were thrown into the streets. Large numbers of workers were moving to places where they hoped they would avoid notice.

Those publications which appeared spoke only in the vaguest terms about the future. All that mattered was the overthrow of Franco and of fascism. In the circumstances, a political party — with a policy dictated from the central committee — would have produced a clear line (however vicious this might be, as the Communist Party's line was after the Stalin-Hitler Pact — one typical symptom being Frank Ryan, I.R.A., C.P. fighter in the International Brigade, who went from Franco's prison to become a Nazi collaborator). The libertarian movement was clear only that it was anti-fascist. And that it would have no further truck with the Communist Party.

This was not an unreasonable line to take in the circumstances, but for a fatal corollary to the anti-fascist commitment, which ultimately paralysed the entire Spanish working-class movement and had kept Franco in power for so long. This was that one must therefore accept anti-fascism at its face-value and ascribe anti-fascism to the democratic powers which happened to be fascist.

A moment's reflection will show the falsity of the position. Today China finds herself in conflict with Russia. But she is not only not necessarily anti-Communist (in the Leninist sense), she is not (in that sense) anti-Communist at all. There is no reason to suppose that if China defeated Russia she would end state dictatorship and concentration camps; to ascribe such motives to China is to deceive oneself deliberately. Neither did it follow in 1939 that anybody who happened to be fighting the Fascist Powers were therefore anti-fascist in the same sense that the libertarians were.

Nor had ideology anything to do with it. America, while retaining democracy at home, is perfectly able to support dictatorship abroad. Yet in 1939 it was seriously supposed even by the best of the Spanish militants that Britain and France must "logically" oppose fascism, as if nations went to war merely to impose their ideology. It was more difficult to support their jailer France, but after France fell, Britain seemed to be sympathetic. The British Secret Service enlisted the aid of the Spanish Resistance groups, which sprang up immediately after the disaster of 1940. They sought aid to bring soldiers out of France over the border; they enlisted the support of the "gangs" inside Spain to raid foreign Embassies and sabotage Nazi plans; they sought to co-operate with (though it never came to dominating) the Spanish resistance in France. Because Franco's men were at the time so violently anti-British, it was supposed Britain must "logically" want to overthrow Franco. And it was more "reasonable" to believe in a British victory — a practical proposition — than in Revolution!

Even those in the Resistance who never trusted the British agents, and who insisted on getting paid for any service they gave them, never believed that they could be double-crossed. Yet after a network of unions had been re-established in Spain during the war — and a Resistance built up without parallel in modern history, inside Spain — all the committees were destroyed. None of the militants ever saw cause and effect. Soon after the war, for instance, a meeting was called by the British Embassy for militants of the C.N.T., to discuss the A.N.F.D. (Alliance of Democratic Forces) and the possibility of co-operation with the (pro-British) monarchists. C.N.T., delegate Cipriano Mera reported that he could not see the point of it. A few weeks later the entire C.N.T., committee was arrested. Cause and effect have not been seen to this day. How could it have been the British Embassy that was the traitor? Britain was "democratic", Franco was "fascist."

One could go on at great length, but it can be seen how the "anti-fascist" period, coming when the union phase had finished, helped to establish a movement in exile, in which no popular representation existed or was required, and acted as a brake on Resistance. After the war, the exiles began to fit into life abroad. What took over their organisation was not a bureaucracy so much as domination by the "names". There was no longer local autonomy in which all met as equals. For a committee in Toulouse, one was asked to pick "names." The "great names" came to the fore. But what were these "great names"? They were not the names of the militants of pre-war days. They were those who came to the fore during the era of government collaboration. Among them was a division

48

on many subjects. Some thought they should enter political collaboration with the Republican Government (pointless now that it was defeated, but it still had money stacked away in Mexico). Others wanted a return to independence – but they could not return to being a union. Only the workers inside Spain could do that.

The majority of exiles never want to compromise their position. It is understandable, but it is fatal for the struggle in the interior. In fact an exile movement is basically in a farcical position, for it is giving up the fact of struggle in the country where it exists and trying to carry one on in a country where it does not exist. It thus surrenders its usefulness as a force in the labour movement in the country where it resides; while at the same time holding back the struggle in the country from which it originates – since the considerations which hold one back from action in a more open society are not necessarily valid in the dictatorship. Time and again, therefore, the Organisation found itself in conflict with the Resistance in Spain, being built up by groups such as those of Sabate, Facerias and others.

The Resistance – because of its daring attacks upon the regime – was able to build up the labour movement time and again. It was destroyed many times; and has been rebuilt. It has expected help from the exile Organisation and received nothing. Worse, it has been held back. For this reason one finds today the whole of the pretended "official" libertarian movement in utter disarray – the Montseny-Isglesias faction expelling all and sundry – striking out in the last gasps of dissolution . . . above all, denouncing the *real* libertarian movement inside Spain because it dares to use the name of the C.N.T! (It is for this reason that organisations like the Federacion Obrera Iberica – to save the recriminations about "forging the seals" of the Organisation which are held as by apostolic succession in Toulouse – have simply changed their name, with the same aims as the C.N.T., of old).

The Spanish Libertarian Movement, socalled (M.L.E.), is not a union movement, nor an anarchist movement. It is anti-fascist in ideology, but basically it looks to a "solution of the Spanish problem" rather than supporting the Resistance in any way. Time and again the expected political solutions have failed – or rather, have succeeded in the way their authors intended them, leaving the M.L.E., pathetically declaring that the British, French or American Governments have let them down. Even now, many cannot understand how it came about that Britain did not send an Army in to liberate Spain; why the Government did not even want to do so – and indeed, that elements in the British Government may have considered Spain already liberated – by Franco! These are the people who denounce the Resistance as "impractical", "utopian" – above all "violent!" Many will explain that "violence" is wrong. That is to say, it was permissible in the Civil War, when it was legal; and during the World War when, if not legal, in Spanish eyes, it was granted the equivalent status by virtue of the fact that resistance *was* "legally" recognised in France, but it became "un-libertarian" even "un-Spanish" with the end of the World War!

This colours the attitude towards Resistance in Spain, and nothing marks a greater dividing line. The Resistance was carefully nourished by the Sabate brothers — of whom so little is known* — the various bands of the Resistance such as the Tallion, Los Manos etc., by Facerias and others. It had perforce to return to the tradition of guerilla warfare and activism.

Despite the "official" propaganda in which the Libertarian Movement in Exile constantly invokes the name of the C.N.T., it is not the same thing at all. The traditions of the C.N.T., are reaffirmed by the Resistance within Spain, which is back in the period of regional committees and local resistance, and is still unable to reconstitute itself on a nation-wide scale — which indeed it may not consider essential.

The period predicted by Marx during which Spanish labour would have to be left to "Bakunin" is, of course, over. The Communists, Maoists and Nationalists of various brands have grown considerably — though socialism and the U.G.T., are dead. Thanks to the folly of "Toulouse" the name of the C N.T., has been eclipsed by schism. But we note one thing: whenever the struggle in Spain becomes acute, the workers turn to anarchism.

*Sabate: Guerrilla Extraordinary, Antonio Tellez, London, 1974, Cienfuegos Press, is now out of print. Facerias, Antonio Tellez, will be published early in 1979 by Cienfuegos Press, Orkney.

What is the C.N.T.?

José Peirats

Jose Peirats is the official historian of the majority labour organisation in Spain, the anarcho-syndicalist **Confederation Nacional del Trabajo.** His magnum opus, **La CNT en la revolucion espanola,** was an unpaid labour of love upon which a number of professional historians of the Spanish Civil War have built their well-paid academic careers. The present study first appeared in **Ruta,** a Spanish language review published in Caracas, and in English in pamphlet form by Simian in 1972 and 1974.

INTRODUCTION

The Confederacion Nacional del Trabajo (the National Federation of Labour) has been a thorn in the side of politicians in Catalonia, and for that matter in the rest of Spain, since its inception (in 1911) right up to the end of the Civil War (in 1939), which was also the end of its open existence. These gentlemen loathed it as a hotbed of organised upheavals in the even tenour of public life, and did not mince their words in choosing the worst epithets they could think of for it.

In the days of the First International, a Spanish Prime Minister, Sagasta, called the predecessor of the C.N.T., the Regional Federation of Spain "a philosophic Utopia of crime;" under the second Republic Azana termed its members "bandits with union cards." Somewhat more objective than either of these gentlemen, the English writer, Gerald Brenan, declared that the anarchist movement in Spain was the most Spanish of all south of the Pyrenees.

Some persons who may have personal reasons for forgetting about the untameable spirit which has historically characterised the Iberian race whether in confrontation with the invader or in opposing a parade of native officiousness, would be better employed than in looking for the origins of anarcho-syndicalism outside Spain. Joint offspring of crude Catalan capitalism and the feudalism of Andalucia, it established itself as a robust movement of protest against political corruption, against an outdated system of landholding, against the plutocrats or the nouveaux riche, and against a narrow-minded ruling class from which Spain has never ceased to suffer.

51

It will be noted that anarchism and anarcho-syndicalism have been spoken of in the same breath. In Spain they are in reality two words which connote the same thing. If there has almost always been a movement called specifically anarchism, with its press and editorials and with other groups attached to it — such as the Libertarian Youth movement, the women's organisations, Anti-fascist Solidarity, clubs, schools etc., — always at the centre of this pulsating swarm has been found the workers' organisation, the C.N.T., the heart of the entire movement as well as its fecund source. The reaction, the bearing, in a word the climate of thinking of the greater part of its component bodies bears the indelible stamp of federaalism, the mark of the C.N.T., for all those who were born of it and died in it were its men.

THE CONSTITUTION OF THE C.N.T.

A revolutionary organisation of the working class such as the C.N.T., cannot be judged by the overt meaning of its constitution. Always in conflict with legality, the C.N.T., found it necessary to have recourse to subterfuges to enable it to obtain the legal recognition which it needed for its trade unions to be able to operate. The rules and regulations submitted to the government only expressed in a summary form what were the principles, tactics and aims of the organisation. Quite often the provincial governors to whom they were sent imposed finishing touches of the text submitted as a condition of according legal authorisation.

As far as our information goes, the rules that can be called characteristic of the movement began to crystallise at the regional congress of the Catalan unions, which was held in Barcelona in June-July 1918.

It was at this congress that the C.N.T., decided that its structure must be based on one single union for each industry. And having done so it went on to lay down the aims of its unionism. A commission at this same congress put forward a draft constitution which was hastily completed afterwards, according to the ups and downs of circumstances. As far as this account is concerned, this was laid down by the commission:—

"An organisation under the name of the Catalan Regional Confederation of Labour has been set up with the following aims and objects: To put into practice the ideal of solidarity between the bodies forming the federation, directed towards the complete emancipation of the working class from monopoly capitalism and from all those who oppose the free development of productive workers. To be prepared to extend its activities, through federal pacts, with similar federations which either already exist or may come into being in the rest of Spain, in Europe and anywhere else in the world."

The second article is concerned with tactics and says:—

"To carry out the foregoing aims, the local and district federations — which shall be the only bodies constituting the Catalan Regional Confederation of Labour, with the exception of such special cases as the trade unions may decide to admit into their fold — shall always struggle in the purely economic field, that is, by direct action, untrammelled by any political or religious prejudice. As regards questions of tactics or procedure, these shall be appraised according to circumstances, even though the action to be taken shall be the preferred mode of combat."

Even though this constitution was formulated by the Catalan Region, the Mentor of modern syndicalism, it was adopted by all the other regional federations of the C.N.T., as can be seen from the following excerpt, for example, from an interesting work by Juan Peiro (The Path of the C.N.T., Barcelona, 1925):

"It is certainly true that the Congress of 1919 laid down that Free Communism is the basic ideology of the C.N.T. . . . . ; but it is no less true that this body, six months after, in submitting its rules for the approval of the (civil) governor of Valencia stated in Article II that in the attainment of these aims the Confederation and its constituent bodies will struggle in the purely economic field, that is by direct action, untrammelled by any political or religious prejudice.' "

Let us note in passing that the 1919 Congress has laid down categorically the use of revolutionary direct action (cf. the records of these two congresses).

The Catalan Regional Congress referred to had discussed thoroughly the question of 'direct action.' It was reluctant to accept such a tactic openly; but nevertheless when submitting its rules to Valencia for approval the criterion of full direct action seems to have won the day, even though it was a matter of lying within the competence of the National Confederation.

Then came 1930, and the end of the dictatorship of Primo de Rivera, which had driven the C.N.T., underground. This time the National Committee sent its rules for approval to the (civil) governor of Barcelona, Despujols. And it was this Despujols, doubtless with the permission of General Mola, Director-general of Intelligence, who signed them after making certain changes which jump to the eyes of an expert. The new text read as follows:—

"An organisation has been set up in Spain under the designation of the C.N.T., which sets out to achieve the following objectives:—

a) To work for the development of the spirit of association among workers, getting them to understand that only in this way can they raise their moral and material condition in modern society, and so prepare the way for their complete emancipation in the conquest of the means of production and consumption.

b) To practice mutual aid between the different bodies in the federation, always when necessary and called for by them, both during strikes and on any other occasion that may arise.

c) To foster relations with all similar working class organisations, whether national or international, with a view to sharing their experiences and thus hasten the total emancipation of workers everywhere.

In Article II is was stated;

"To carry out the foregoing aims, the Confederation and the trade unions which are its constituent bodies shall confine their struggle to the purely economic field, and shall resolve their differences with those concerned directly; with the bourgeois, such as may be of an economic nature; and those of a social kind or concerning public order and services with the government or with the departments concerned, freeing themselves completely of any political or religious alignment."

DIRECT ACTION

During the regional congress of 1919 an interesting discussion took place on the subject of the tactics to be followed. Should the movement base itself on direct action, multiple action or a mixture of the two? On this proposition, the platform issued the following directive: "Even though the principles which inform the regional federation are based on the doctrines of revolutionary syndicalism and its tactics, there exist in its midst some unions which do not carry on their struggle with Capital in this spirit and even act on a multiple base, we recommend that the Congress resolves that no bodies should belong to the Confederation which do not accept in its full extent the principles of direct action."

In course of debate it was evident that although no-one, or almost none, was against direct action, the emphasis with which the platform put forward its recommendations did not take into account, in the opinion of some, the backwardness of many workers. If the principle of direct action was accepted in all its rigour, such workers would implicitly find themselves outside the organisation. Even Juan Peiro himself, who might be considered the most representative theoretician of Spanish revolutionary syndicalism, took the view that a declaration of principles should be made which was not so extreme as that contained in the motion before congress. He said: "Direct action, even if accepted by all of us, has not yet been absorbed thoroughly by any but small groups. Hence the acceptance of the motion would result in the exclusion from the Confederation of many forces which already accept direct action in principle, even though it is not felt dogmatically."

In the end Congress resolved: "In the battle between Capital and Labour, those unions belonging to the Federation are under the obligation of adopting by preference the system of direct action in circumstances of real gravity, they do not call for the use of other distinct formulas."

In the upshot, as we have seen, the constitution of the C.N.T., was characterised — at least when not deleted by the governors, as happened with Despujols — purely and simply by the statement that the tactics of the C.N.T., were to be direct action.

In practice, there was a certain amount of confusion. Direct action came into conflict with the alleged impartiality of the government when arbitrating in conflicts between Capital and Labour. Revolutionary syndicalism well understood that, far from being neutral between employers and workers, the authorities were fiercely allied with the capitalists, since they had a host of common interests which bound them to the side of the 'bosses'. Their awards were necessarily, it followed, against the interests of the working class.

If the authorities confused direct action with violence, certain militants who were not sufficiently instructed thought it a mortal sin if a strike committee paid a visit to the government offices. In this respect, if the rules established in 1930 leave out mention of direct action, in turn they define it perfectly by stating that conflicts between capital and labour shall be settled directly, with the employers, while those of a social nature or having to do with the services shall be taken up with the authorities.

54

"ONE UNION"

"One Union" as defined by the same Congress of 1918, is not what its sworn enemies have been propagating about it. With *mala fides*, they allege that it discloses a wish for monopoly; One Union means a Single Union (for all). The sole monopolists are those totalitarian regimes which have imposed a single monopolist union, shackling employers and workers together by decree in something which is proclaimed to be the end of the class struggle without abolishing the classes.

The idea of a single union for each industry ("One Union") was not invented by the 1918 congress. In the first workers' congress, that of June 1870, a form of organisation was adopted, which when perfected the following year at Valencia evoked the admiration of the internationalists who met in London that same year around Karl Marx (he will be mentioned again later).

Let us note in passing that in every period of reorganisation after a spell more or less prolonged of suppression, the working class militant is faced with the fragmentation resulting from different workers' groups in the same place of work, ironically called "chapels." This is to say that, in the same locality, there are to be found different groups of carpenters, or locksmiths, or smelters, run by little local "bosses" who defend their petty fiefs against the syndicalist organisation with cloak-and-dagger tactics.

The "One Union" came to put an end to such gangster-chiefs. And in doing so, it ended their parochial quarrels and emphasised the unity of the working class. Further, the "One Union" carried the federalist enterprise to the furthest extent, spreading it throughout the region and the whole country. For all that, the One Union was already in existence in Barcelona before 1918.

INDUSTRIAL FEDERATIONS

Anselmo Lorenzo recalls in his "The Proletarian Militant" the defence which Garcia Meneses made of the Report on Organisation. The movement was at that time developing in two parallel directions. On the one hand, on the grounds of solidarity, of the defence and of militant education, the basic units — the 'locals' — were federating themselves into local, district and regional organisations of all trades mixed; but apart from this at the same time the 'locals' of each separate trade were joining themselves together to form federations of the same industry on a local district and regional basis. In this way, during the last century, the Council of the Spanish Regional Federation had to take on the duty of representing both federal structures; the same had to be undertaken by the National Committee of the C.N.T.

The Federation of the different trades unions came into being in 1911 as someone recalled at the 1918 Congress: "It was at the last Congress held (in 1910) at the Bellas Artes Palace (in Barcelona) that the lines and outlines were traced along which were to be modelled the national organisations of the working class. It was in this congress that it was agreed, and that in no uncertain terms, to direct workers' unions to form themselves on a basis of a federation of 'locals' in the same industry in regional and national groupings being the only units that were to make up the Grand Confederation of Workers."

"It was on the basis of this decision," said the speaker, that was formed the Metallurgical Federation, "which was a local one to begin with, but later became a regional one, resulting ultimately in the formation of the National Metallurgical Federation." (Reminiscences of the 1918 Congress of Catalonia, Toulouse, 1957). But this same 1918 Congress left in the air the necessity for the formation of the federations in each kind of trade. Their resolution was as follows: "It is not considered useful to form federations in each trade on a national scale, but as this question falls within the competence of a national congress of the C.N.T., it is left to such a congress to resolve it.

The next national congress, that of December 1919, dropped such trade unions from its plans, but those already in existence refused to dissolve themselves. Not only that, but other trades federated themselves on a national basis, such as the telephone workers, and those in the oil industry.

From the moment the Second Republic was declared (1931), there began a renewed interest in the question of federating within each kind of industry. As the advocates of the system were the German anarcho-syndicalists, an outstanding Spanish militant sarcastically observed that these federations were being imported into Spain "inside a barrel of beer."

Juan Peiro, the champion of Federations of Industry, was to write: "In our opinion, it was a grave error of judgement which the Congress at the Comedy Theatre (Madrid, 1931) made in agreeing to the abolition of federations of locals on a basis of a nationwide industry. Their existence was in no way incompatible with the existence of those called 'one union. groupings . . . It is true that some of the trades federations in being at the time were over-centralising, being at fault in sucking dry the individuality of the local unions of which they were composed; but this should not have been a reason for breaking them up . . .

To national organisations of the bourgeoisie there should undoubtedly correspond national organisations of the working class, grouped according to industries . . . Otherwise, it is not possible to confront or resist the capitalists. The general tendency of bourgeois capitalism, we have pointed out many times, does not limit itself to an economic-industrial concentration, nor even to the formation of national federations; their objectives go far beyond such limits and seek to find them, and already begin to find them, in international organisations and understandings. It would be absurd to agree for one moment that such a state does not call for a corresponding economic-industrial purpose in the defence of the productive class." (Anarcho-syndicalist Themes, Barcelona, 1930).

The national congress of 1931 after a long and passionate debate, accepted the industrial superstructure, but the split that occured the same year put off an agreement to such an uncertain future that the most fervent advocates of a new formula abandoned the organisation. When in 1937 at long last the industrial federation began to be reformed it was too late. The C.N.T., had scarcely any time left to run.

OBJECTIVES OF THE C.N.T.

The federal congress of 1919 declared that the aim of the C.N.T., in accordance with the essence of the principles of the (First) Workers' International, is Free Communism." However, since at the time there was

56

adopted another motion to join the Third International provisionally, some may draw the conclusion that the Free Communism of the C.N.T., and the Soviets were one and the same.

Soviet communism derives ultimately from the "Communist Manifesto" of Marx and Engels; free communism descends from the doctrines developed by Peter Kropotkin in his book "The Conquest of Bread." Here are two conceptions fundamentally opposed to each other.

The Russians seek to build communism by means of the Dictatorship of the Proletariat. Free Communists are opposed to any authoritative body, and consider that it is possible to bring about socialism directly, without any dictatorship, for socialism without freedom is not socialism at all, neither can despotism ever lead to liberty. They trust in the social forces inbuilt in Man, which will rise to the surface and grow when oppression by the state and by capitalism ceases, and through the enjoyment in common of the sources of natural wealth and of the means of production.

REVOLUTIONARY SYNDICALISM

The C.N.T., calls itself revolutionary syndicalist because it is a fighting organisation both in the immediate present and with the prospect of overthrowing the State through armed revolution by means of a revolutionary general strike. Revolutionary, too, because through its own bodies located in the centres of production and its federal organisations such as the trade union and its agro-industrial co-operatives, it considers itself capable of taking over the tasks of production and of distribution after the revolution has taken place.

With vistas of ambitious projects such as these Peiro assigned a most important role to the industrial federations, which were to prepare themselves beforehand by learning the economics and technology, the application of technological developments to industry, the fluctuations of supply and demand, the statistics of export and import etc. In the factories, the shop stewards' committees of today, fighting for the interests of their union members in the place where they work, should become tomorrow the technical committees who will administer the enterprises in a socialised economy.

The same Peiro gave a very important part in a socialist economy to the existing consumers' co-operatives as centres of distribution in the future: "The distribution of produce will similarly hold as important a role in the society of tomorrow as the articulation of production. This, not so much in respect of the development of production, exactly, as because organised distribution will be a factor in the orientation of the people from the first moment of the Revolution as far as the provision of food is concerned — we all know already how much the triumph of the revolution depends on this. That is why, further, that the Co-operatives have to be unfailing in their function as the means of distribution in the new society freed from the trammels of Capitalism and the State.

THE QUESTION OF FEDERALISM

Both the Unions, in the thick of the class war and also the industrial federations and co-operatives in a constructive age of revolution, regard federalism as their driving force. Libertarian communism has within its hold trade unions, industrial federations, co-operative societies and free

57

communes (municipalities). In fact, the word *Communism* is derived from the commune or municipality. In the Iberian peninsula, there is a tradition of independent public charters, and free communes of the Middle Ages.

Politically and administratively, most Spanish libertarian communists thought of the commune as a self-governing unit capable of federating itself with other similar units, that it to say, sovereign within its own boundaries, but linked by a free pact with its neighbours. Federation always implies the freedom and self-government of the federating bodies, but this does not mean their independence.

Pi y Margall, who has been the moving spirit of Spanish anarchism as much as, or perhaps even more, than Bakunin or Kropotkin (for beginning with Salvochea and Mella, many Iberian anarchists drew their inspiration from him), has written in his book, *"Nationalities"*: "Federation comes from the Latin word *foedus*, which signifies an alliance or compact; it cannot be arrived at without the contracting parties being free, that is to say, *sui juris*." He added, on the subject of the municipalities of the Middle Ages: "The citizens not content with their *fueros* or own law codes, attempted all the time to extract further privileges to buttress them. If for any reason they united with their neighbours, it was to defend local freedoms, even against the king himself, whom they always looked at with cautious and suspicious eyes. With this sole aim, there were organised chiefly in Castille and in Leon, those famous brotherhoods or groups which were so powerful in the last third of the Middle Ages, and unfortunately went down with Juan Padilla at Villalar. They acquired great power in this fashion, and so far from being for the benefit of the State, brought the State into their service."

In the C.N.T., before the Civil War, all decisions to act were taken in a meeting of the branch, whether in an office or a factory. There it was that the tasks were laid on the men who were to carry them out. In general, these jobs were not renumerated. In this there was a scrupulous tradition no less rigourously followed. Because of this rule, it was difficult to turn the militants into bureaucrats, since they were regularly replaced at the end of their term of office, usually annual, and so did not come to feel like functionaries. This sacred custom was only broken during the three years of war. This bureaucracy, being carried over into the exiled organisations, became a bad habit and led to deplorable consequences, bureaucracy led to an acute crisis for federalism, and to an asphyxiating growth of centralism.

Under normal circumstances, the federal organs are the local federation, which is the grouping of all the union 'locals' in an important centre of industry, or the One Union, which links together all the agro-industrial 'locals' of a district. Then come the District Committees, the regional committees and the National Committee. Deliberative bodies are in the following line: the assemblies of all affiliated bodies – which in times when the C.N.T., is functioning 'underground' are replaced by meetings of the militants; the regional or national congresses, in which direct representatives of the previously mentioned assemblies take part, being summoned to discuss a 'slate' the motions forming which have been selected by the basic units themselves; the plenary sessions, which cannot, however, discuss fundamental propositions, which are the prerogative of the congresses, nor can they modify resolutions agreed to at the latter; finally the conferences, which are empowered to discuss fundamental themes, but have to submit the propositions agreed to, however, to the referendum of the individual unions.

Resolutions can be adopted by acclamation if no dissentient voice is raised against them; but normally voting by a majority is required ('majority law'), or by proportional representation, dropping progressively a certain number of votes for every one thousand members represented. Proportional voting was established to prevent the small unions from the villages being crushed by the huge concentrations of members in the capital. At congresses and at grand plenums, where the unions are directly represented, committee members have no voting rights, cannot put forward resolutions, nor present reports on their own behalf. They can only intervene of their own accord to announce that such and such a previous agreement is being contravened, or to inform the assembly of their activities.

APOLITICISM OF THE C.N.T.

Following a line which goes back to the days of the First International the C.N.T., proclaims its complete independence of all political parties. The congress of 1918, so often referred to in this account laid down that 'professional politicians can never represent workers organisations, and the latter should make sure that they never affiliate themselves to any political club.' We have already seen that by its constitution the C.N.T., must "fight in the purely economic field, untrammeled by any political or religious prejudice." Although any wage earner, whatever his political or religious notions, could belong to the C.N.T., no one could represent it who had appeared as a candidate in any local or parliamentary elections, or who had accepted political undertakings.

Faithful to the principles of revolutionary syndicalism, as proclaimed by the French C.G.T., at its 1906 Congress, the C.N.T., set itself to develop by acting outside political and parliamentary institutions. Its energies were directed to strengthening the unions, to organising industry, and to preparing its affiliates on a techno professional basis in its revolutionary setting.

Fundamentally, all politicians were alike, those of the left as much as those of the right, above all in their approach to power. They all made the same promises and undertakings to the public at the beginning of their career and on the eve of elections. They all turned their coats in the same manner, betrayed their principles and rode roughshod over their electors once they got into office. Since they are incapable of altering their nature, these judgements took on the character of dogmas in the C.N.T. It can be said that as time went on and with the growth of the movement outwards – in 1919 its membership reached one million – it was due solely to the discovery made for themselves by the workers that such growth came about.

Democracy became defined, no less sarcastically, as a lure to "catch the unwary", a sleeping draught, or an iron for deformed limbs, twisted by the contradictions of capitalism.

It provided no solution for the fundamental problems of the capitalist system – the division of society into exploiters and the exploited – neither in the municipalities nor in the councils nor in the parliaments. The very commune itself, so close to the life of the people, had been turned into an engine of oppression, used to collect taxes and to select conscripts for the army.

The militant literature of the C.N.T., distinguishes between authoritarian socialists and communists on the one hand, and those who do not limit themselves to anticapitalist demagogy, but attack the State as well, because they believe it to be the source of all evils. It is from this attitude that all those anarchist anathemas against power find a loud-speaker in the C.N.T: there is no such thing as revolutionary power, for all power is reactionary by nature: power corrupts both those who exercise it and those over whom it is exercised; those who think they can conquer the State in order to destroy it arc unaware that the State overcomes all its conquerors; there are r o good and bad politicians, only bad ones and worse; provisional governments turn into permanent ones inevitably; the best government is no government at all; the Nation is not the People, nor is the State the same as Society; instead of the government of men, let us have the administration of things, peace to men, and war on institutions; dictatorship of the proletariat is dictatorship without the proletariat and against them; to vote for politicians is to renounce ones own personality; your union is yourself: if you find that society is bad, you are there to improve it . . . . . and a thousand other aphorisms.

THE C.N.T. AND THE COMMUNISTS

At the height of the Russian Revolution when the Bolsheviks were employing anarchistic phraseology (which hid their real aims at seizing and holding on to power), the C.N.T., allowed itself to be led astray into joining the Third International. At that time, the Entente had set about broadcasting the most tendentious 'news' about Russia, and thereby stimulated the sympathies of proletarians the world over in favour of the great Russian people who had overthrown the legendary tyranny of the Czars. All the same, the C.N.T., announced its adherence with reservations. It was to be provisional, and subject to the outcome of an enquiry on the spot by a representative, and to the decisions of a World Congress to be held in Spain, at which a true Workers' International was to be set up.

In 1920, a delegate was sent to Russia who took part in the second Congress of the Third International. On his return, he declared that under the pretext of revolutionary power there had been set up in Russia the naked dictatorship of a single party. As soon as the C.N.T., was able to meet after the frightful repression of 1920-22, it broke completely with Moscow, which evoked against it the hatred of Cain on the part of the Bolsheviks and of such few disciples as they had been able to find in Spain.

It can be stated without fear of denial that it was the C.N.T., who first unmasked in Spain the new gang of Czars in Russia, who behind their revolutionary mask were able to poison the stream of old liberalism in Europe, and to break up the former centres of trade unionism by means of a disruptive and centralising policy at the service of the foreign interests of the totalitarian Russian State.

The U.S.S.R., invested untold financial resources in Spain, and was lavish with the number of its agents: it made use of the venal spirits with persistence, for the purpose of conquering by every means possible the powerful centres of revolution in Spain. But they broke their teeth on a proletariat deeply imbued by the C.N.T., with the principles of one of the most original philosophies of liberty.

Just before the Civil War broke out, the communists had the luck to penetrate the U.G.T., which they found ideologically unarmed, and whose Youth movement they were able to take over at the beginning of the war. From this party base, the gains they made through the Popular Front in the February 1936 elections, and those provided for them by the black-mail of Russian aid to the Republic during the war, was initiated the totalitarian enterprise which avorted the promising popular rising of July 19th, 1936.

Finding anarcho-syndicalism the chief obstacle in the path of their ambition to take over the Republic, they used every possible means to destroy it, leading to a series of provocations which culminated in the furious battle of May 1937 in Catalonia. After this, the C.N.T., lost in a maze of negotiations a battle it had won on the barricades against the communists, masterminded by the O.G.P.U., and their eventual allies, the assault guards of the Generalitat. But even though they had to undergo the humiliation of seeing their collectives destroyed by stormtroopers of the stalinist military chiefs, heroes of the baseline, the C.N.T., had sufficient resources in reserve to touch off the last episode of the war, an offensive of all liberal elements against those who till the very last moment were waging war for and on behalf of Moscow.

HISTORICAL SUMMARY

The C.N.T., is the successor of the Spanish section of the First International which with ups and downs lasted from 1868 down to 1910. From its first congress in 1911, the C.N.T., remained 'underground' until 1914. In 1916, together with the U.G.T., it called for a general strike against shortages of food. In August 1917, again in common with the U.G.T., it brought about a revolutionary general strike. In 1918, it is seen re-organising itself in industry-wide unions. In 1919 was unchained the most complete general strike in the history of the Spanish working class, against the 'Canadian' group of industries who had the full support of the civil and military authorities in Catalonia. The same year saw a disastrous lock-out by the bourgeoisie, at the very moment when in Madrid was being proclaimed that the aim of the C.N.T., was Libertarian Communism. At this juncture it numbered one million members.

During the years 1920-22, the C.N.T., resisted heroically the repression let loose by the 'Viceroy' Martinez Anido, the despotic governor of Barcelona. Its militants were hunted through the streets of the capital and shot down like animals. They returned blow for blow, and in their turn fell two ex-governors and one Prime Minister (Eduardo Dato). During the dictatorship of Primo de Rivera (1923-30), a 'health cure' was effected in secrecy, the C.N.T., participating in all the conspiracies against the monarchy.

In 1930 the C.N.T., surfaced. Its first trumpet call was the appearance of "Solidaridad Obrera" (Workers' Unity) as a daily. The king fled and the Republic arrived. Would the C.N.T., be allowed to consolidate itself? Both the Home Minister (Miguel Maura) and the Labour Minister (Largo Caballero) persecuted it: the first with his assault troopers, the second with his coercive laws, such as mixed tribunals and compulsory arbitration. The majority decided to set in motion the processes of revolution. A minority withdrew itself from this activity.

At the beginning of 1932 there was a preliminary uprising in the Catalan Pyrenees. The government replied with deporting those taking part to Spanish Equatorial Africa. In August of that same year, the C.N.T., helped to stifle the 'pronunciamento' of General Sanjurjo in Seville. 1933 opened with a more extensive uprising in Catalonia, Andalucia and the Levante (East Coast). It was put down with the utmost cruelty in an Andalucian village, where 'Seisdedos' (Sixfingers) and some of his associates were besieged in a shepherd's hut and burnt alive by the Guardia Civil.

Because of these oppressive measures, the C.N.T., waged a vast anti-parliamentary campaign during the elections of November 1933, in consequence of which the Republican-Socialist coalition lost, and the Right parties formed the new government. Against both right and left the C.N.T., let loose yet another insurrection, which reached its greatest intensity in Aragon and the Rioja district. In October 1934 the C.N.T., and the U.G.T., jointly brought about an uprising in the Asturias, which was liquidated at the cost of hundreds murdered and 9000 sent up for trial. Under the protection of an amnesty, the C.N.T., took part in the campaign for the next general election, which took place in February, 1936. The C.N.T., observed a calculated objectivity, which this time contributed to the victory of the Popular Front. Lastly in July of the same year, the C.N.T., triumphantly put down in Barcelona the officers' rising against the Republic, and so made it possible to offer a prolonged resistance to their revolt during the Civil War.

During that tragic period, there were three main stages:
1. By the immediate impulse of the victorious resistance in the streets, the most warlike militants took the road towards the combat front, at first as columns of militiamen, subsequently as units of the People's Army.

2. Those militants experienced in the day-to-day organisation and running of unions understood that the hour had struck to put into practice the economic transformation foreseen in the term libertarian.

3. The top cadres of the movement acknowledged the crushing weight of a situation which they had been incapable of foreseeing seriously. They never outgrew their apprenticeship in which, paradoxically, they had to act the unwelcome part of acting as a brake on the inexperienced revolutionary impulses of their own comrades. They had to take on an ungrateful task, for which they were neither prepared not felt a vocation.

Apart from the epic tale of the barricades and the trenches the most glorious page in the history of the C.N.T., was written by the anonymous membership which manned the industrial and agricultural communes. Expropriating those who were fascists and uniting the petty parcels of land owned by small peasants, the C.N.T., decided to work them collectively. They put into practice the free exchange of products, so far as they were permitted by the obstruction of the bureaucracy, or by the punitive squads sent out by the counter-revolutionary communists.

62

In the centres of industry, hundreds of businesses were collectivised, and there were established small workshops which were left to continue on their own but were brought into the sphere of practicality. Plans of advanced socialisation such as the formation of the Timber Collective of Barcelona, or the Union of the cowherds and the bakers of the same district, were fulfilled at last. The heroism of the workers in these collectives could be gauged not only by the constructive capacity of which difficulties were surmounted in course of their unaccustomed burdens. For everything was against them: the atmosphere of war, the backwardness of the peasantry, whether large or small, the malice of petty civil servants whose jobs had been reduced in importance or were about to be abolished, the obstruction offered by the old governing class as they increasingly began to raise their heads again, the all-embracing network of regulations and ukases which they issued, lastly, the hounding by the assault troops and officers of the regular army.

THE HUMAN MATERIAL OF THE C.N.T.

Before all else, let us pay a tribute to the militant, who always has been the inexhaustible source of strength of the movement. In general, his name never appears in its publications, and scarcely ever in the rollcalls of its congresses. His sphere of action has ever been the union branch, the district assembly, the committee listening to highly excitable workers' claims, the bargaining table facing the employer, the strike committee etc.

In normal times, this very struggle gave birth to militants in large numbers, by reason of the opportunity it offered the man of good will and spontaneity. But, above all, it created the fighting material, the traditional repudiation of servility and of mercenary work. The militants were the soul of the organisation, its nervous system and its blood vessels.

Then there were the militants whom one could call those of the top rank. They emerged from the mass of militants mentioned above, and took on the heaviest responsibilities in the local union branches, the federation's committees and in the industry-wide union offices. They did not thereby become a separate class of workers, it being borne in mind that they turned up daily at their place of work, whether field, factory or mine, and carried out their devoted labour of love outside working hours. An old tradition, become established law, laid down that no-one could belong to the C.N.T., who did not work for a wage and have an employer. This little rule was a barrier which shut out self-employed workers, those belonging to co-operatives, intellectuals and some kinds of technicians.

Much later, when unions had been set up for the liberal professions and for intellectuals, the door was opened to workers by brain as well as those by hand. In many ways these new recruits to the movement were looked on with suspicion by the older membership. Those who joined with the *arriere pensee* to find some self-advantage in the C.N.T., soon discovered that because of the critical atmosphere surrounding them, and the lack of any messianical spirit, this was not the organisation for them.

As regards the highly qualified technicians, they sought shelter in the C.N.T., for other than merely speculative reasons. An organisation ever in the thick of the battle, under a constant hail of blows aimed at it by the Government, was not able to offer them anything other than the reward of imprisonment or an occasion to shed their blood. It was because of this circumstance that the white-collar workers retreated into their quiet self-important little strongholds. The C.N.T., suffered from a double allergy: that which it inspired in these gentry, and that which they elicited from it.

To those intellectuals who had been forged within the movement, and had acquired thereby an iron will, there were held out only the vicissitudes of the struggle and the joys of secret literature. These self-taught heroes ran and edited newspapers and reviews, essayed the writing of books, novels, poems and speeches, and taught in schools as well.

There is no more than a mere sketch of that important aspect of Spanish life which was the C.N.T. To obtain a more complete idea of it, recourse must be had to the enormous literature of the movement, of the multitudinous piles of newspapers and reviews that give the real feel of an organisation which was above all a never-failing dynamism in the service of a great idea, which embraced both illusion and sacrifice.

CRITICAL AFTERWORD

There are in Peirat's work a few strands of thought which do not bear close analysis. We may dismiss as naive his belief that State Communism derives from the 'Communist Manifesto' (in which there is no mention of dictatorship and little with which anarchists would disagree) while anarchism derives from 'The Conquest of Bread' (a socialistic exposition which does not deal in any way with the differences between State and Free Socialism).

This in any case contradicts his beliefs that Spanish anarchism is 'Spanish' and one should not look for its roots elsewhere. The same belief in the 'national origins' of anarchism is expressed by Rudolph Rocker (in 'Anarcho-Syndicalism' he gives it entirely English origins), Voltarine de Cleyre (in 'Anarchism and American Traditions' gives it American origins) and Lui Shih-pei, who assumes it to be of Chinese origin (see 'Origins of the Anarchist Movement in China'). No doubt all are right. But nothing could be more 'Spanish' than the Roman Church and that was, to a large extent, an 'import.'

It may also be questioned whether, even if the Spanish capitalists and government had been more liberal, the workers would have compromised with them. But the study remains a fascinating introduction to the one labour movement in Western Europe that resisted equally Capitalism, Reformism and Stalinism.

64

Self Management in Action

Gaston Leval

The following three essays on anarchist self-management in action are small extracts from Gaston Leval's richly detailed study of collectivisation in Spain during the Civil War. The book is an indispensable and very readable source for all interested in the practice of anarchism (it is also an unrepeatable bargain at present costs!) **Collectives in the Spanish Revolution**, Gaston Leval, translated by Vernon Richards, 368pp, £2.00, Freedom Press, London.

LIBERTARIAN DEMOCRACY

There was, in the organisation set in motion by the Spanish Revolution and by the libertarian movement, which was its mainspring, a structuring from the bottom to the top, which corresponds to a real federation and true democracy. It is true that deviations can occur at the top and at all levels; that authoritarian individuals can transform, or seek to transform, delegation into intangible authoritarian power. And nobody can affirm that this danger will never arise. But the situation was quite different from what it is or would be in a State apparatus. In the State which Marx when he was seeking to court favour with the Paris Communards who had escaped the slaughter, so as to win them over to his cause, called a "parasitic superstructure" of society men installed in positions of command who are inaccessible to the people. They can legislate, take decisions, give orders, make the choice for everybody without consulting those who will have to undergo the consequences of their decisions: they are the masters. The freedom which they apply is *their* freedom to do things in the way they want, thanks to the apparatus of law, rules and repression that they control, and at the end of which there are the prisons, penal settlements, concentration camps and executions. The U.S.S.R., and the satellite countries are tragic examples of this.

The non-Statist system does not allow these deviations because the controlling and co-ordinating *Comites*, clearly indispensable, do not go outside the organisation that has chosen them, *they remain in their midst,* always controllable by and accessible to the members. If any individuals contradict by their actions their mandates, it is possible to call them to order, to reprimand them, to replace them. It is only by and in such a system that the "majority lays down the law."

65

Since 1870 this system had been adopted by the Spanish libertarians, who, in their determination that the mass of members should pronounce and decide for themselves as often as possible on the problems that arose as well as on the running of activities were following the ideas of Proudhon and Bakunin.

Did this mean that there were no minorities, no individuals exerting an often decisive influence on the assembly, or in the daily life of the Syndicates, Collectives, Federations? To answer in the affirmative would be to lie and would deceive nobody. As everywhere and always, there were in those organisms militants who were better prepared, who were the first to stand in the breach, and to preach by example, risking their own skins, and who, driven by the spirit of devotion and sacrifice, were better informed on the problems, and found solutions to them more readily. The hist ry of mankind concedes a worthy place to the minorities who have assumed the responsibility for the happiness of their contemporaries and the progress of the species. But the libertarian minority assumed that role according to anti-authoritarian principles, and by opposing the domination of man by man.

To emancipate the people it is first of all necessary to teach them, to push them to think and to want. The sizeable and enthusiastic libertarian minority sought therefore, as we have seen, to teach the masses to do without leaders and masters and to that end were always communicating information to them, educating them, accustoming them to understand the problems affecting them either directly or indirectly, to seek and to find satisfactory solutions. The syndical assemblies were the expression and the practice of libertarian democracy, a democracy having nothing in common with the democracy of Athens where the citizens discussed and disputed for days on end on the Agora; where factions, clan rivalries, ambitions, personalities conflicted; where, in view of the social inequalities precious time was lost in interminable wrangles. Here a modern Aristophenes would have had no reason to write the equivalent of *The Clouds*.

Normally those periodic meetings would not last more than a few hours. They dealt with concrete, precise subjects concretely and precisely. And all who had something to say could express themselves. The *Comite* presented the new problems that had arisen since the previous assembly, the results obtained by the application of such and such a resolution on the volume of production, the increase or decrease of any particular speciality, relations with other syndicates, production returns from the various workshops or factories. All this was the subject of reports and discussion. Then the assembly would nominate the commissions; the members of these commission discussed between themselves what solutions to adopt; if there was disagreement, a majority report and a minority report would be prepared.

This took place in *all* the syndicates *throughout* Spain, in all trades and *all* industries, in assemblies which, in Barcelona, from the very beginning of our movement brought together hundreds or thousands of workers depending on the strength of the organisations. So much so that the awareness of the duties, responsibilities of each spread all the time to a determining and decisive degree.

The practice of this democracy also extended to the agricultural regions. We have seen how, from the beginning of the Civil War and of the Revolution the decision to nominate a local management *Comite* for the villages was taken by general meetings of the inhabitants of villages, how the delegates in the different essential tasks which demanded an indispensable co-ordination of activities were proposed and elected by the whole assembled population. But it is worth adding and underlining that in *all* the collectivised villages and all the partially collectivised villages, in the 400 Collectives in Aragon, in the 900 in the Levante region, in the 300 in the Castilian region, to mention only the large groupings which comprised at least 60% of "republican" Spain's agriculture, the population was called together weekly, fortnightly or monthly and kept fully informed of everything concerning the commonweal.

This writer was present at a number of these assemblies in Aragon, where the reports on the various questions making up the agenda allowed the inhabitants to know, to so understand, and to feel so mentally integrated in society, to so participate in the management of public affairs, in the responsibilities, that the recriminations, the tensions which always occur when the power of decision is entrusted to a few individuals, be they democratically elected without the possibility of objecting did not happen there. The assemblies were public, the objections, the proposals publicly discussed, everybody being free, as in the syndical assemblies to participate in the discussions, to criticise, propose etc. Democracy extended to the whole of social life. In most cases even the individualists could take part in the deliberations. They were given the same hearing as the collectivists.

This principle and practice were extended to the discussions in the municipal Councils in the small towns and even in sizeable ones – such as Villanueva y Geltur, Castellon de la Plana, Gerona, Alicante or Alcoy. We have seen that when, because of the exigencies of war, our comrades had joined these Councils, as a minority, they nevertheless very often exercised an influence far greater than their numerical strength, firstly because they secured the agreement of the other parties, who could not easily refuse, that discussions should be open to the public. Ordinary people with free time made a point of attending them. And often social reforms of immediate value (building of schools, nurseries, children's playgrounds, decent conditions for the old) were snatched from the political majority which would not have been granted if the discussions had taken place behind closed doors.

Both at the individual and local levels, we think these different aspects of libertarian democracy ushered in a new civilisation. To give a more exact idea of what is meant, we will observe the unfolding of a village assembly in Tamarite de Litera, in the province of Huesca, at which the writer was present.

The *pregonero* (public crier) presents himself at the cross roads, in the square and at the busiest corners of the village. He blows three times on his small horn with which he always announces his presence, then in a slow, light tenor voice which, for some reason I do not know, is used by all *pregoneros* in Aragon, he reads, clipping the words and sentences somewhat at random, from a paper on which is written that the members of the Collective are invited by the administrative Commission to attend the general assembly which will take place that same evening at 9 o'clock.

At 9.30 p.m. the local cinema is half full. At 10 p.m. it is packed. There are about 600 people including some 100 women, girls and a few children.

While waiting for the opening of the meeting, everybody is talking without shouting in spite of the expansive temperament of the inhabitants of that region. In the end the secretary of the Collective mounts the platform alone. Silence falls and the secretary immediately proposes the adoption of necessary arrangements:

"We must," he says, "nominate a secretariat for the meeting." Immediately one of those present asks to speak "on a point of order."

"There are some individuals in the hall. They are enemies of the Collective. They have no business being here, we must turn them out. What's m re, it is imperative that women should remain silent during the discussion, otherwise they will have to be removed as well.

Some of those present seem to be in agreement with the double proposal; others clearly have doubts. The secretary replies that in his opinion the individuals should be allowed to remain and even take part in the discussions. "We have nothing to hide and it is by seeing how we act that they will end by being convinced." As to the talkative women – they are peasant women who had never attended such discussions before and who also have a right to speak – they will surely keep quiet and there will be no need to have recourse to such extreme measures. The assembly approves and the individuals remain.

Then the secretariat is nominated, consisting of comrades who are elected in turn. Then the chairman speaks. He is, naturally, one of the most active militants, and one of the best infromed on the problems included in the agenda. He starts by dealing exhaustively with the reason for the Commission calling the extraordinary assembly. Though intelligent, he is no speaker, but makes a great effort to express himself with the utmost clarity and succeeds.

First question: Four comrades on the Commission must be replaced because they are not carrying out their tasks satisfactorily, not through any bad will on their part, but because they lack the necessary background. Furthermore, there is a certain amount of discontent with the delegate dealing with food supplies. He is very able but has a difficult personality and his manner is too brusque, which results in unpleasant confrontations, particularly in inter-regional relations; it would perhaps be better if in future he dealt with the barter arrangements with more distant regions where individual contacts are not so important. The delegate for industry and commerce could look after the distribution at local level, and the relations which this involves with members of the Collective.

The assembly accepts, without unnecessary discussion, the changes recommended and nominates successors. Then the delegate for food supplies has his duties limited in one direction and extended in another.

Another question which is on the agenda: A fairly large group of members of the Collective have just recently withdrawn from it to return to individualist activities. But the Collective which has taken over non-agricultural local production possesses all the bakehouses for breadmaking and the individualists' group claims one.

68

Faces are serious, concentrated, tense. Women make their comments without raising their voices. A collectivist has the floor:

"We must lend them a bakehouse for a fortnight or a month to give them time to build one for themselves."

"No," replies another, "they should have remained with us. Since they have left us, let them get on with it!"

A third declares that there are already too many bakehouses in the village and one must not build any more. Many other members expressed themselves with that economy of words which is a characteristic of the Aragonese peasants. When nobody else wishes to speak then the chairman expresses his opinion.

In the first place there is the problem of the smooth running of the economy. To construct another bakehouse is to waste material needed for other uses; it will in due course involve an expense for wood and electricity, which must be avoided, for the repercussions of bad management do not rebound only on the individualists but also on the whole national economy. Now, we must show that we can do better than the capitalists. This is why, instead of increasing the number of bakehouses being used we must even reduce them. Let us therefore make the bread ourselves and for the individualists. But they will supply us with the amount of flour required to make the amount of bread they need and there will be the same quality of bread for all of us. Besides, we must not refuse bread to the insividualists for, in spite of their error they must be in a position to eat, and in a situation in which the present roles were to be reversed, we would be happy if our adversaries did not prevent the collectivists from feeding themselves.

The chairman has convinced the assembly, which following the comments of some collectivists, approves without dissentients.

The next question concerns the pros and cons of rationing bread. The high family wages paid by the Collective allows them to buy large quantities, which encourages some abuse, and even sometimes inequalities which the Revolution cannot permit. Consequently it is necessary to establish a top limit for consumption to ensure that every family can obtain the quantities it needs without there being waste.

The assembly accepts the rationing, but then a juridical problem is posed: who will apply the measures decided upon, the municipal Council or the Collective? The former covers the whole population; the individualists, who represent an eighth, and the Collectivists. If the municipal Council takes charge, rationing will have to be established for everybody. If it's the Collective, the individualists will not consider themselves obliged to respect it. Many views are put forward which allow for an assessment of the powers of the two organisations. And it is decided to ask first the municipal Council to undertake the task. If it does not accept, the Collective will − at least within the limits of its possibilities.

But the withdrawal of the individualists has posed another problem. Many of them have left their old parents on the hands of the Collective, while at the same time setting themselves up on the land which formerly belonged to the old folk they have now abandoned. Those dispossessed have been taken care of by the Collective because they are old and unable to work, but the behaviour of those individualists is unacceptable. What action can be taken?

The chairman, who has outlined the dispute, makes it quite clear from the start that there is no question of expelling the odl folk. In any event they will be assisted, but their children must take back their parents or forfeit their land. Such is his opinion.

A number of members of the assembly take part in an orderly manner throughout. One suggests that the irresponsible sons should be deprived of half their harvest. Another repeats that it would be a shame to oblige these old folk to leave the Collective: anything must be considered but that. They return to the suggestion made by the chairman: either the individualists take their parents to live with them or they will have no land and solidarity of any kind will be withheld from them. The moral issue is uppermost. The proposal is approved.

Every time a solution is approved and before another is taken up, the assembly comments, giving free expression to its thoughts. Nevertheless the general conversation is not noisy, and barely lasts a minute.

Now the question to be discussed concerns the potteries which in normal times were a source of revenue as they supplied many villages in the region and even some small towns with jugs, porous water coolers and *cantaros* (earthenware pitchers). They also manufactured tiles and bricks there. But as there was a shortage of manpower in the fields because of the mobilisation for the front, the potters were sent there and abandoned the potteries; others too were at the front. Thus production had fallen off sharply. What should be done?

One man suggests that the potters should work a ten hour day instead of eight; another that one should increase the manpower in the potteries; a solution supported by a third speaker who adds that they should try to bring in skilled men from other regions. He also suggests that the tile factory which had been closed as a result of the current situation, should be reopened.

He is given the reply that we are in a war situation and that one can do very well without tiles. Laughter from the assembly, which approves, and as someone asks why cannot the skilled workers produce this year as much as in the previous year, the secretary of the Collective, a former mayor and who is well informed on these matters, explains that before many cantons obtained their supplies from Huesca and since this town is now in Francoist hands, they get their supplies from Tamarite. One must get the potters to return to their craft and in addition we must put an appeal in our Press for skilled workers from other regions to come and live here. Proposal accepted.

They have come to the end of the agenda, and move on th "any other business." One of the members points out that in Tamarite there is an *alpagatero* (a canvas shoe maker) who is good at his job. One could organise a workshop where the women could go and work instead of wasting their time gossiping in the street. The women laugh, but the proposal is accepted. A man of between 50 and 60 points out that the little girls of the village are not serious, since they prefer to go out instead of going to work in the workshop specially set up for them to learn dress-making. As a solution to the problem he suggests that a good dressmaker be selected with the task of training them, but that the classes should be held in a church without windows. The door would be bolted and the little girls not allowed out during the working hours. Everybody laughs, the parties concerned more than the others.

Many collectivists express their views in turn, and it is decided that in every workshop a woman delegate shall supervise the apprentices. Those who do not attend on two consecutive occasions without good cause will be dismissed. But the man who would have kept them under lock and key is implacable; he suggests quite seriously, or so it seemed, that to punish them when their work was unsatisfactory the young girls should be made to fast for two or three days. To that there is a general roar of laughter.

New problem: The nomination of a new hospital director (and we learn that the director is a woman, which is fairly unusual). This hospital has been converted into an Old People's Home, but they are now being treated at home by a doctor who joined the Collective and the cantonal hospital is at their disposal for all urgent cases or serious illnesses. This again poses a problem of jurisdiction. It is a general hospital. It is a question of ascertaining whether or not it comes under the municipal Council reconstituted following the publication of the decree emanating from the Valencia government. If it does, the hospital is everybody's responsibility, collectivists and individualists, and the latter must also share in the expenses. So far the Collective have paid everything and its enemies have taken advantage of its bounty. A matter for further study.

Following the examination of questions of less importance the chairman closes the session. The assembly has lasted 2½ hours. Most of those who took part were peasants from the village or its environs, accustomed to rise early, and who at that time of the year had worked twelve or fourteen hours.

Yet no one left before the end of the discussions, not even those who had remained standing as there were not enough seats to go round. No woman or child had gone to sleep. Eyes had remained wide open, and faces as wide awake. One read on them, at the end, as much, often amused, interest as one had observed at the beginning. And the chairman, at the same time paternal, fraternal and the teacher, had to insist to prevent a much longer agenda.

The final resolution adopted concerned the frequency of assemblies which from being held monthly were to take place weekly.

And the collectivists made their different ways home to bed commenting on the discussions and resolutions adopted as they went. Some lived a fair distance away and travelled either on foot or on bicycles.

WATER, GAS AND ELECTRICITY IN CATALONIA

The workers' Syndicate which from the beginning of the Revolution guaranteed the supply or production of drinking water, gas and electricity in Catalonia had been founded in 1927 under, and in spite of, the dictatorship of General Primo de Rivera. Others had been started throughout Spain, and the federation of these industries was set up in the canton of Barcelona. Next appeared the Catalan regional Federation and finally uniting all the regional federations constituted in Spain, the national Federation, the secretariat of which was set up in Madrid.

No doubt this structure was facilitated, and encouraged by the nature of the production, especially electricity mainly from hydraulic power* and based on the exploitation of the heads of water from the Pyrenees or of barrages situated at great distances — sometimes hundreds of kilometres — from the transformer stations and the distribution centres.

On a national scale, most workers joined promptly. In Barcelona the C.N.T. Syndicate had normally between 2,500 and 3,000 members, and 7,000 in the whole of Catalonia. Then after 19th July, in the new situation created by the Revolution, workers and technicians together numbered 8,000. For its part the U.G.T., had a little less than that number, in Catalonia that is.

The technicians, semi-technicians, and establishment had set up their own Syndicate independent of the two workers' organisations. But the vitality of the solidarity sprung from the Revolution drove them towards closer union with the manual workers, a necessary union for maintaining production. And an assembly resolved, by acclamation, to dissolve the separate Syndicate and to constitute the technical section of the single Syndicate affiliated to the C.N.T. Later ideological preferences came into play and fifty of these technicians left the C.N.T., to form a section with membership of the U.G'T.

The directors of the power stations who earned anything up to 33,000 pesetas a month while the workers earned less than 250 were mostly foreigners. They received orders from their Consulates to return home. Meanwhile, thanks to the efforts of all workers, and in spite of a lack of some technical staff of international origin, water, gas and electricity continued to be supplied right until the end of the Civil War. Only the bombardments caused temporary breaks in supply.

The initiative in the early days did not come only from our Syndicate as the constituted organism. Just as for the tramways and railways, it came from militants knowing how to shoulder responsibilities. The very day of the Francoist uprising, a handful of them were meeting to guarantee the continuation of these public services. Immediately works *Comites* were set up as well as a central liaison *Comite* between the two workers' organisations. Later this *Comite* supervised the general organisation of work and production for the four Catalan provinces of Barcelona, Tarragona, Lerida and Gerona.

The definite take-over did not occur until the end of August 1936. During the transitional period, of about six weeks, they were prepared to continue production with the existing capitalist organisation, without attempting expropriation. Every worker remained at his job as before; major decisions, which involved a taking over of a technical-administrative nature, were taken by syndical assemblies of the two workers' organisations. And the curious thing was, though it happened on other occasions, that not only did the Syndicates take over the organisation of work to be done from the capitalists, but they assumed the responsibilities that the latter had previously undertaken. Thus it was that they took over the financial commitments and the debts from their predecessors, and paid all

---

*Before 1936 the production of electricity for the whole of Spain had for years remained at about 3,000 million k.w., all from hydraulic power sources. A great number of barrages were later constructed but it was realised a little late in the day that they only filled to about a third of their capacity. It therefore became necessary to intensify thermic production.

the invoices, undoubtedly in order not to jeopardise workers employed by the suppliers, and who were also inheriting the situation as bequeathed to them by their employers.

The only debts that were cancelled were the obligations to Spanish moneylenders, most of them privileged people — small savings were to all intents and purposes non-existent in Spain. What money people had was used to acquire some of the necessities they badly needed.

At the beginning of 1937, total income had dropped by 20%. Possibly some consumers had omitted to pay their bills, but there was also another explanation. The unit price of electricity had been reduced; some water rates had risen from 0.70 to 0.80 pesetas a cubic metre and in other cases had dropped from 1.50 to a standard tariff of 0.40 pesetas. And there was no longer a meter charge.

Naturally the attitude of workers in the U.G.T., was combated by the politicians who were at the head of the reformist Union. But their stubborn opposition could not breach the resolve of members, and agreements continued to reign among all workers.

The system of organisation that was put into operation encouraged this good understanding. Its point of departure was at the place of work, at the undertaking, and rose to the Syndicate. We will take a closer look at how things worked.

In the undertaking itself, the first nucleus is the job speciality. Each speciality sets up a section immediately with groupings by factory, workshop or "building" of at least 15 workers. When there are not the numbers to do so, workers from many trades collaborating among themselves, meet and constitutes a general section. The sections are more or less numerous and varied, depending on the size of the factories or of the organisations. Each section nominates two delegates which the assemblies choose: one of a technical calibre who will participate in the *Comite* of the undertaking, and another entrusted with the management of work in the section.

The "building *Comite*" (as it is called) comes next. It is nominated by the section Commissions and consists of a technician, a manual worker and an administrator. When deemed necessary a fourth member is nominated so that the two syndical organisations shall have equal representation.

The manual workers' delegate has to solve, or try to solve, difficulties which might arise between different sections, those arising within a section being settled by the interested parties themselves. He receives suggestions from workers in the different trades for the nomination or the transfer of personnel. And the sections give him daily reports on the progress of work.

He also acts as go between for the rank and file and the general Council for Industry. Periodically he calls the sections to general meetings which take place at the Syndicate, which tightens the links between the workers from the different undertakings. During these meetings proposals and initiatives are studied which are likely to improve productivity and production, as well as the workers' situation, or be of interest to the syndical organisation. A copy of the deliberations is sent to the Council for Industry. It should be noted that the specific activities of the manual workers' delegate do not prevent him from continuing to work at his job alongside his comrades.

The delegate with administrative functions supervises the arrival and warehousing of materials, records requirements, deals with book-keeping for supplies and reserves, and keeps an eye on the state of income and expenditure. He also deals with correspondence and it is his responsibility to see that balance sheets and Reports addressed to the Council for Industry are prepared.

The delegate with technical functions supervises the activities of his section, and uses every endeavour to increase productivity, to lighten the workers' burden by introducing new methods. He checks on production at the power stations, the state of the network, prepares statistics and charts indicating how production is developing.

Let us now examine more closely the workings of the Councils of Industry at the summit of the organisation.

There are of course three; one each for water, gas and electricity. Each is composed of eight delegates; four for the U.G.T., and four for the C.N.T. Half of those delegates are nominated by general assemblies of of syndicates,* the other half by delegates of the technical sections in agreement with the central *Comite*. This latter measure has as its objective to ensure, in the composition of the Councils for Industry, the nomination of men who are technically and professionally suitable, which I was told does not always happen in syndical assemblies where oratorical gifts, ideological or personal affinities can relegate the more necessary considerations to secondary importance. All this is capped by the general Council of the three industries, which is also composed of eight members with, as before, four from each union organisation. This Council co-ordinates the activities of the three industries, attunes the production and distribution of raw materials from a regional, national and international point of view, modifies prices, organises general administration, indeed takes and uses all initiatives bearing on the producers' production and needs as a whole. Meanwhile, it is obliged at all times to submit its activities to the scrutiny of local and regional syndical assemblies.

Let us now examine the results of this example of workers' management. From a technical point of view some achievements deserve to be underlined, such as that most basic one of all which we constantly come across, of concentration and of co-ordination.

Not all the stations, by a long chalk, were as important as those of Tremp and Camarása which are the main generating stations fed by large barrages. Apart from these two giants, most of the 610 units (including the transformers) dotted all over Catalonia had a small or insignificant output; to keep them in operation suited some private interests, but the public interest hardly at all. It was necessary to link them, to eliminate and to reorganise which is what was done. Six months after socialisation had begun 70% of stations representing 90% of output constituted a perfectly homogeneous technical whole; and 30% which represented but 1% of this output were kept apart.

Among other things this represented a saving in labour which was used on improvements and alterations often of importance. For instance 700 workers constructed a barrage near Flix which increased the available electricity by 50,000 k.w.

*Because of dispersal of the personnel in production units throughout Catalonia the question poses itself as to how the general assemblies nominated these delegates. And we must admit to not having enquired into this point when we were gathering material for this study.

Gas production was economically less important, and I did not gather statistics on the subject comparable with my researches into electrical power. The more so as the growing lack of coal due to the sea blockade made it impossible to make noteworthy improvements in production.

By contrast water, especially drinking water, the supply of which required a large and costly organisation, generally for every tenant in every apartment, was never lacking even in the towns that had suffered bombing raids. In Barcelona the daily supply of 140,000 cubic metres before the Revolution rose rapidly to 150,000 and went on increasing. Nevertheless the increase was not great for it was not easy in a region so broken up, to set about creating new catchment areas, all the sources having long ago been put to use.

THE BARCELONA TRAMWAYS

The tramways were the most important means of transport in Barcelona. Sixty routes criss-crossed the city and served the suburbs and the surrounding localities: Pueblo Nueva, Horta, Sarria, Badalona, Sens, etc. The General Tramways Company was a private company mainly with Belgian capital and employed 7,000 workers, not only as drivers and conductors but also in the eight tram depots and in the repair workshops.

Out of the 7,000, about 6,500 were paid up members of the C.N.T., where they made up the section of the industrial transport Syndicate corresponding to their occupation. The other, much less important, sections were from the underground (two lines), the taxis which in due course created their own Collective, the buses and, finally, the two funicular railways of Montjuich and Tibidabo.*

The street battles had brought all traffic to a standstill, obstructed the roadways by barricades that had been set up all over the city and for which buses and trams often were the main materials used. The roads had to be cleared, and public transport so indispensable for this large city had to be got moving again. So the syndical section of the tramways appointed a commission of seven comrades to occupy the administrative offices whilst others inspected the tracks and drew up a plan of clearing work that needed to be done.

In front of the offices of the company the Commission found a picket of civil guards who had been instructed to prevent access. The sergeant in charge declared having received orders to let no one pass. Armed with guns and grenades, and some of them well protected in the armoured car which the company used for transporting money, our comrades adopted a threatening attitude. The sergeant phoned his superiors for suthorisation to withdraw and this was agreed to.

One must stress one small detail which has something quite piquant about it. All the top level personnel had left, and the syndical delegation found in the offices only the lawyer instructed to represent the company and to parley with them. Comrade Sanches, a leading militant, the most active and experienced of them, knew that gentleman only too well for two years before he had sentenced our comrade to 17 years in prison · following a strike that had lasted twenty-eight months; the defender of the

*A mountain rising to 580 m. its lower slopes covered with pines, dominates Barcelona.

75

interests of the company had actually demanded a sentence totalling 105 years in prison.* This gentleman received him most cordially, declaring that he accepted the new situation, and even that, as a lawyer, he was putting himself at the service of the workers. Sanchez' comrades wanted to shoot him on the spot but he was opposed to that. He even gave the personage permission to withdraw. It was Friday and an appointment was made with him for the following Monday. His confidence restored, the man asked to be accompanied to his house as there were rather a lot of armed revolutionaries in the streets . . . He was escorted, but the following Monday did not show up. He was not seen again.

The *Comite* of seven immediately called together the delegates from the different syndical sections: electric power station, cables, repairs, traffic, conductors, stores, accounts, offices and administration, etc. Yet once more the synchronisation of the industrial Syndicate was working perfectly. It was unanimously agreed to get the tramways moving without delay.

The following day a call was made over the radio — as the engineers had already done for their members — calling manual workers and technicians. Most of them responded; known fascists kept away. All the engineers put themselves at the disposal of the Syndicate, including a former colonel whose active sympathy for the workers had resulted in his demotion from the head of the traffic section and director of the Metro to a job in the archives section.

Five days after fighting had stopped seven hundred tramcars instead of the usual six hundred, all painted in the colours of the C.N.T.-F.A.I., in red and black diagonally across the sides, were operating in Barcelona. The number had been increased in order to do away with the trailer-cars which were the cause of many accidents. To do this work had gone on night and day repairing and putting back into service a hundred tramcars which had been discarded as being beyond repair.

Naturally things could be organised so quickly and well because the men involved were themselves well organised. One finds here therefore an *ensemble* of sections constituted by trades and put on an industrial base, according to the organisation of the work to be done, of the enterprise of the Syndicate. Drivers, conductors, repairers, joiners, etc., as many complementary groupings going beyond the simple traditional professional cadre, and brought together in a single organisation.

Each section had at its head an engineer nominated by agreement with the Syndicates, and a representative of the workers and this was how the work and the workers were dealt with. At the top the assembled delegates constituted the local general *Comite*. The sections met separately when it was a question of their specific activities which could be considered independently; when it was a question of general problems, all the workers of all the trades held a general assembly. From the bottom to the top the organisation was federalist, and in this way they maintained not only a permanent material solidarity but also a moral solidarity which linked everyone to the general task, with a nobler vision of things.

*Sanchez had come out of prison with thousands of other comrades as a result of the amnesty granted after the elections of February 1936.

Agreement was therefore also permanent between engineers and workers. No engineer could take an important decision without consulting the local *Comite*, not only because he agreed that responsibility should be shared but also because often, where practical problems are invovled, manual workers have the experience which technicians lack. This was understood by both parties, and thereafter, very often when the *Comite* of the Syndicate or a delegate thought up an interesting idea, the specialist engineer would becalled in for consultations; on other occasions it was the engineer who proposed the examination of a new idea and in that case manual workers were called in. There was complete collaboration.

It was not enough to put the tramcars, even in larger numbers back onto the tracks, not just to repaint them in the colours of the Revolution. The different corporations decided to carry out this additional work without any overtime pay. The creative drive dominated all. In the sheds there were always twenty or thirty tramcars being checked and done up.

The technical organisations and the traffic operation was improved; the importance of the improvements achieved was remarkable. To start with, 3,000 metal poles holding up the electric cables supplying the current were eliminated as they were interfering with the traffic and causing many accidents and were replaced by a system of aerial suspension. Then a new safety and signalling system was introduced consisting of electric points and automatic discs. Furthermore the company for *Agua Luz y Fuerza* (water, light and power) had installed in many places and right in the middle of the routes taken by the tramcars, transformer cabins or power distributors, which made all kinds of detours and bifurcations necessary, sometimes very sharp (and very often a single line), and resulted in accidents. This had gone on from when the services had first been laid, and were determined by the whims of financial or political interests. The comrades of *Agua, Luz y Fuerza* moved these cabins to where they would be in nobody's way, thus making it possible to straighten out once and for all the tramway lines.

Sections of track that had been demaged during the fighting were reconstructed, such as the double track for Route 60 which was completely relaid. In other cases the roadway was asphalted.

These improvements took some time to complete as did some modifications of the general infrastructure. From the beginning the organisers, without for all that forgetting the interests of the workers in the vast enterprise, sought to perfect the tools being used. In less than a year a number of notable acquisitions were made; first of all there was the purchase in France of an automatic American lathe, the only one in Spain, and costing £20,000, which was able to produce seven identical parts at the same time.

Two ultra modern milling machines, and electric warning machines one to be notified of breakdowns and broken cables; new cables replaced the old. And an electric furnace was bought for melting down bearings. Much more technical equipment was thus purchased, including Belgian electrode welding sets for use on the tracks which cost the then high price of £25,000.

Thus tooled it was possible to make appreciable strides forward, and a start was even made on building tramcars, including two new models of funicular cars for the Rebasada line which climbed the Tibidabo and for the one in Montjuich.* The new cars weighed 21 tons compared with 35 tons for the old type which also carried fewer passengers.

Before that the whole system of power supply had been reorganised and the dynamos repaired.

*

Let us take a brief look at the financial results of the new organisation. Some figures were supplied to us by the principal organisers of this revolutionary creation; we have obtained other, official, figures published in the workers' press at that time. They go from September 1936 when the accountancy was taken in hand and the figures can be relied on.

TOTAL MONTHLY INCOME

	1935	1936
September	2,277,774 *pesetas*	2,600,226 *pesetas*
October	2,425,272	2,700,688
November	2,311,745	2,543,665 ·
December	2,356,670	2,653,930

The monthly increase in receipts varied between 12% and 15%, and it might be thought that the increase was the result of an increase in fares. Not so, for steps were actually taken to lower fares in general. Formerly they were based on distance and varied from 0.10 to 0.40 pesetas. In September a uniform charge of 0.20 pesetas was made which mainly benefitted workers who lived on the outskirts and had been paying the higher rate, and especially those who had to pay the night rates.*

Such reductions in fares would have resulted in losses under the previous administration, but the suppression of capitalist profit and of high salaries for the administrative executives and technicians actually made it possible to show an operating surplus.

*

The balance sheet of services rendered is equally positive. During the year 1936 the number of passengers carried was 183,543,516. The following year it had gone up by 50 million to 233,557,506 passengers. This is not all, for the kilometres covered also increased from 21.7 million to 23.3 million, an increase of 1.6 million kilometres.

It must be recognised of course that these figures can in part be explained by the growing shortage of petrol for motor vehicles as a result of the blockade of the Spanish coasts. Nevertheless the fact is that the new organisation was able to provide an answer, and more, to the growing needs of the public.

To get there they did not have to be satisfied with continuing along capitalist lines; much more had to be done. They did so, even more so than would appear from the brief outline given here. For before the Revolution the workshops of the Tramways Company of Barcelona manufactured only 2% of the material used, and generally speaking were

*A hill in Barcelona dominated by a fortress where Francisco Ferrer was executed in 1909.

†The first increase took place twenty months after the beginning of the Revolution. This was the result of the increase in the prices of raw materials and the cost of living, which involved wage increases.

set up to deal only with urgent repairs. The tramways sections of the workers' Syndicate for communications and transport of Barcelona, in its eagerness to work, reorganised and improved the workshops which at the end of the year were producing 98% of the materials used. *In a year* the proportion had been reversed, in spite of an increase of 150% in the price of raw materials which were getting more and more scarce, or coming from abroad at exorbitant prices.

And not only did the tramway workers of Barcelona not live on the reserves of capitalism, as the detractors of collectivisations, or syndicalisations, maintain or imply, but had to deal with financial difficulties they inherited from capitalism, as did the Syndicate in the textile industry of Alcoy, and the shoe factory in Elda. On July 20th, while the battle still raged, the tramworkers' wages, amounting to 295,535 pesetas, had to be paid (they were paid every ten days). Shortly afterwards bills totalling 1,272,528 pesetas for materials previously purchased by the company had to be paid. And up to the end of 1936 general operational expenses amounting to 2,056,206 pesetas were paid, a further 100,000 pesetas for medical services and accident benefits, 72,168 pesetas in bonuses for economies made in powder and materials — a scheme operated by the old company; finally 20,445 pesetas in insurance payments for staff.*

Nothing was overlooked. It is true that we are not yet at the stage of complete and completely humanist socialisation of the agricultural Collectives, with the application of the principle "to each according to his needs." But we cannot repeat too often that in the towns the republican regime with State institutions had not been, and could not be abolished; that a fair proportion of the bourgeoisie and the traditional political currents still exsited, that it had not been possible to socialise commerce. It was inevitable that even the most daring achievements should feel the effects of this. Nevertheless what was done by syndical socialisations was in itself far reaching.

For the spirit of the workers of Barcelona and other cities such as Valencia was probably the most likely in the whole world to bring about economic equality and the application of mutual aid. It was thus that both in order to help them to meet temporary difficulties and to contribute to their development, the tramways section of Barcelona financially assisted other sections of urban transport. The buses received 865,212 pesetas, the funicular lines of Tibidabo and Montjuich 75,000, Barcelona port transport 100,000 and the Metro undertaking 400,000. And on December 31st, 1936 the Barcelona tramways had 3.3 million pesetas in hand.   *

An odd fact: not only did the Spanish libertarian workers agree to settle with suppliers all debts contracted by the company, but they also wanted to deal with the shareholders. There must have been quite a

---

*To these sums must be added taxes which other socialised undertakings also paid. The Valencia central government demanded 3% on the gross receipts; but the Catalan Government, with its seat in Barcelona, demanded what it had been previously receiving from the foreign capitalist company: no less than 14 different taxes which made a total of 4 million pesetas. The Syndicate requested a meeting with the government and after minor discussions agreement was reached with a lump sum payment of 1½ million pesetas.

number of them, the capital consisting of 250,000 shares of 500 pesetas, but they probably all lived abroad. Our comrades by means of posters and press announcements invited shareholders to a general assembly. Only one, a middle-aged woman, who owned 250 shares turned up. Quite unalarmed by events, she declared herself satisfied to entrust the management of her small capital to the workers' Syndicate with whom she would henceforth maintain relations of trust. I do not know the end of this story but if the woman had no other resources I would be surprised to learn that she had been deprived of all her means of support. Such inhumanity was not common among our comrades.

*

It now remains to see what part of the profits went to the tramway workers. At the time of the uprising the *peones* (labourers) earned between 8 and 9 pesetas a day, traffic controllers received 10, lorry drivers, and skilled engineering workers (lathe operators, fitters, etc) 12. All wages were readjusted so that labourers received 15 pesetas and skilled workers 16. One was approaching a state of basic equality.

But other improvements in working conditions deserve to be mentioned. Firstly washbasins were installed in the sheds and workshops, which had never been done before. Showers were installed (and one should bear in mind that this was 1936) in all undertakings employing numbers of workers. Tramcars were disinfected weekly. Then a medical service was organised from which we can draw some lessons.

This service was based on the division of Barcelona and its surrounding districts into thirty sectors. A doctor was in charge of each sector and was paid by the Tramways Syndicate of Barcelona. These doctors did not only treat tramway workers but their families as well. A home help service was also set up, the members of which looked after the sick and brought them human warmth, advice, moral support, all those things which often are more needed than medical treatment itself. At the same time, it was used for checking up on possible malingerers — one had not yet attained human perfection. When it did happen — and it was not often for the outlook was not what it was under capitalism — the Syndicate took steps which could go as far as withholding a week's money. Normally a sick person received his full wage.*

To this organisation of home helps was added the use of a fine clinic which until then had been available only to the rich. Apart from being comfortably appointed in contrast with the traditional hospitals in Barcelona, the walls were repainted, decorations provided, radios installed, specialised treatment was provided by a gynaecologist, a specialist in the digestive tracts, a specialist in general surgery. All three were working in the service of the Syndicate.

*Work discipline about which the new social order was, generally speaking, more strict because there was a concern not to fail, but to prove a greater administrative ability and greater production, was to be found also in the tramways syndicate, whose decisions in the cases of drunkenness, very rare and deeply repugnant to Spaniards, were always taken in general assemblies. The steps taken would consist in suspension from work and the man's pay would be handed to his wife, for several weeks, thus giving her the possibility to exercise her rights to deal with the household budget.

Spontaneous discipline, workers' morality, were recognised by all. There was support of, and participation in, the common task, and efforts were constantly made to sharpen the imagination to find technical improvements and new methods of work. In the different workshops "ideal boxes" were put up so that anybody with an idea could submit it in writing.

This participation even went beyond the framework of the undertaking and of the Syndicate. As they were well tooled the workshops produced rockets and howitzers for the Aragon front. The workers worked overtime without pay and even came in on Sundays to do their share for the common struggle, without pay.

To conclude this aspect of things, it is worth underlining that honesty was general. Not that there were no cases of unscrupulous actions but in three years they amounted to six cases of larceny which would not even deserve to be mentioned but for the fact that we do not wish to appear to gloss over the negative aspects. The most serious case was that of a worker who from time to time took away small quantities of copper which he would sell when he had made up a kilo's worth. He was dismissed, but as his wife came to tell the undertaking's *comite* that she had a child which would suffer the consequences, she was given three or four weeks' wages and her husband was moved into another workshop.

Spain: The Re-emergence of Revolutionary Syndicalism

Andrew Giles-Peters

Preamble

There is a popular theory that Spain is not quite European; that
Africa begins at the Pyrenees. And indeed the Iberian dictatorships
seemed less of a European than of a South American (or Hispanic) type.
Unaffected by the Second World War and the destruction of European
fascism as a world-historical force, benefitting from rather than being
troubled by the Cold War, the Iberian dictatorships survived into the
seventies without serious internal threat. Then within a few years of
the deaths of their respective figureheads they were transformed officially
into democracies, by the time-honoured hispanic process of military coup
in the one case and as a gift of the new monarch in the other. Thus it
would be very tempting to write off the current changes in Spain as a
more controlled version of the Portuguese experience.

It would however be premature to do so since there is another theory
originating with Marx and further developed in the 1930s by Karl Korsch
that better explains the nature and possibilities of the current Spanish
situation. Briefly the theory is that Spain experiences all the revolutionary convulsions that pass through the European continent but later, with
increased amplitude and for a more prolonged period. As Korsch
showed this explains why the predominant tendency in the working-
class movement became the revolutionary one of anarcho-syndicalism
rather than the reformist one of marxian social-democracy.[1] It also
explains the development leading to the working class's assumption of
power in parts of Spain in 1936 and why it was that communism could
only become a significant force by leading the attack on the revolutionary section of the working class. It also gives us a key to the analysis of
the present period which may in certain respects be regarded as a
repetition[2] both of the 1930-31 transition from the de Rivera dictatorship to a bourgeois democratic republic and of the earlier period of the
introduction of anarchism to Spain (1868-82).

82

I

The radical wave of the sixties, which received perhaps its highest expression in the French student revolt and general strike of 1968, had at that time only weak echoes in Spain. However the developments of that period – in particular the steady leftwards movement of catholic trade unionism, most notably in South America, Quebec, France and Italy but also in Holland and other countries – extended from the early sixties to the mid-seventies with Italy in particular going through a much more profound radical development than France, though at a slower pace and somewhat later. These developments not only led to the re-emergence of a significant left opposition to the communist parties, but also to a breaking of the monopoly held by these parties on ·vorker radicalism in the countries where they were strong. Since the sixties the pace in radical action in the working class has been made by workers independently of the unions or by the non-communist, and usually ex-catholic, unions.

Whilst these events had their echoes in Spain at the time they by no means ended there. The Spanish 'sixties' extend rather right up to today and possibly for some years to come. A consequence of the deadening weight of a dictatorship extending from cultural and intellectual to political and union life was that only small groups could participate at all in the general European movement at the time and it is only with the death of Franco in 1975 that large masses of the people have entered at all into political, union, or cultural activity of a previously oppositional nature. The seventies in Spain were the most conflictive years for the dictatorship since the guerrilla campaigns of the forties and the death of France and transition to a "democratic" monarchy have opened the way to increasing popular ferment.

If Spain is still in the ascending phase of a "sixties" style movement – or perhaps has arrived now at its zenith – what can we expect of developments there? One thing that can be said is that developments in Spain will proceed rather differently from those in the rest of Europe. For this three main reason can be adduced. Firstly, the Spanish union organisations, which were only legalised from 28 April 1977, are all small by European standards and are divided between six national and two regionalist federations. Secondly, the Spanish revolutionary left – leninist, trotskyist, maoist (including ex-catholic) and basque nationalist – is large and relatively well organised and influential by European standards. The Communist Party (PCE) however is small compared with the other "mediterranean" Communist parties even if large by Spanish standards.[3] Thirdly, the historical organisation of the revolutionary working class in Spain – and Spain is perhaps the only European country to have had such a working class – was the anarcho-syndicalist Confederacion Nacional del Trabajo (CNT – National Confederation of

Labour) rather than the Communist Party and the CNT, illegal from 1939 to 8 May 1977 and subject until 1976 to rigorous repression, is now rebuilding itself in Spain. Thus the replay of the European events of the 1960s/early 70s, which in Europe led to the clear decision by most communist parties for classical social democracy (the "Eurocommunist" phenomenon) and to the emergence of smaller militant leninist and maoist organisation to their left, cannot have the same results in Spain. The PCE i s indeed pursuing eurocommunist strategies but despite its continued existence through the years of clandestinity it is not clear that it yet has deep roots in popular life. On the one hand it faces marxist-leninist competitors deeply implanted in particular regions, e.g. the trotskyists and revolutionary nationalists in the Basque country and the maoists in Aragon and Catalonia; on the other hand it is faced by the possibility of a mass resurgence of anarcho-syndicalism, particularly in Catalonia and Valencia. Under these conditions the strategy of respectability – which depends on the control of the large masses of the working class in order to be able to put a brake on outburst of militancy – can hardly be successful. Once again then Spain will prove to have the more profound radical development since the crisis of the 1960s was also a crisis of – and a phase in the decomposition of – the classical stalinist parties. However if in Spain the European crisis of the late 1920s led to proletarian revolution in Catalonia and Aragon in 1936 what can we hope of the European crisis of the 1960s?

II

Until 1976 it was fashionable to write Spanish anarchism off as one of the world's great, albeit interesting, failures. Even for those who bothered to follow its history beyond 1939 when the bulk of the anarchists went into exile it hardly seemed hopeful. The anarchists fought a guerrilla war against the new dictatorship whose history is only now coming available.[4] They also tried to keep the CNT in underground existence in Spain and by 1950 had built up a substantial union organisation with 50,000 members in Barcelona alone. However the carnage of the civil war, the mass emigration of 1939, the mass executions of the early 1940s and the regular murders and arrests thereafter obviously weakened the CNT and the underground CNT was gradually destroyed by the dissension within the CNT-in-exile and by increased repression against the underground unionists in the late 1940s and early 1950s. A full twenty national committees of the CNT were arrested in Spain during the Franquist period as were also several regional committees including the important Catalan regional committee. Once substantial police operations were launched against the union it was only a matter of time before the major committees were captured since of necessity even underground trade unions are still relatively open organisations. The other factor negatively reacting on the underground CNT was the division in the exile CNT between a majority following policies of republican alliances and counting on international action against Franco and an activist minority practising guerrilla raids over the French border into Catalonia. Neither of these helped, and in fact both hindered, the development of a mass workers' organisation underground in Spain. By 1976 very little of the old CNT was left after 40 years of a dictatorship which, to the anarchists at least, preserved to the end an implacable face.

However in early 1976* the CNT re-emerged with a national meeting of 700 in Madrid followed by a regional meeting of 400 in Barcelona. Throughout 1976 the new national committee worked to organise regional committees — that of the Basque region, for example, being set up by 15 people on 15 September 1976 — and then early in 1977 a trial public meeting of 4,000 people was held in the Catalan city of Mataro followed on 27 March by a big public rally of some 25,000 - 30,000 near Madrid, still under formal illegality. The membership of the CNT was also growing rapidly; from perhaps 10 -15,000 at the beginning of 1977 to 20,000 - 30,000 in March and 40,000 in May. Since its legalisation on 8 May 1977 the CNT has undoubtedly grown further and has held further large meetings culminating in late July with a three day cultural festival in Barcelona which attracted some 300,000 to 500,000 people. What such figures as these indicate however is not clear since relation-shops between the numbers of members and sympathisers (or merely interested people) vary between regions as do the membership growth rates. Thus the CNT of Euskadi (the Basque lands) had grown from its initial 15 in September 1976 to some 1,000 by May 1977 and its journal *Euskadi Confederal* had a print run of 8,000 while the national and Catalan CNT journals had distributions approximately equal to the respective membership numbers. This plainly indicates growth potential in Euskadi but one should not assume stagnation elsewhere: the CNT recorded a 400 per cent membership increase in Catalonia for the first three months of 1977. By comparison the growth rate in Madrid is much smaller: from some 1,500 in March (when the CNT attracted over 25,000 to its rally) to 3,000 in May (when the CNT attracted some 6,000[5] to a heavily repressed illegal May Day demonstration). The impact of legalisation on all this is hard to predict: palinly many more people will feel safe in attending CNT meetings; the CNT press, hitherto distributed clandestinely, will be able to be distributed openly and perhaps by commercial channels; the CNT will be able to organise openly, which

---

* re-emergence of the CNT. The author dates this as early 1976. But this was only when it became possible to come out of hiding following the death of Franco in late 1975. As early as 1973 militants of the CNT of the interior were claiming a strength approaching that of the (by then) comparable period of clandestinity under Primo de Rivera. (ed. note).

is particularly important in Andalusia, an old stronghold, where the CNT was still disorganised and in deep clandestinity in 1977, but one cannot say the degree to which this will lead to further dramatic gains in membership.

The CNT will clearly grow further but it must be remembered that the above are still small numbers by CNT standards. At its peak the CNT had some one and a half million members (in the Republican-held part of Spain in 1936-37 and in the equivalent period to the current one between the fall of the dictatorship and the birth of the Republic in 1930-31 it had some ten times its membership in May 1977. On the other hand in 1931 the CNT's main union opposition, the socialist-led Union General de Trabajadores (General Workers' Union), had been legal during the dictatorship and actively encouraged by the quasi-fascist regime of Primo de Rivera (as it was later by the republican regime). Thus the famous socialist trade union leader Largo Caballero was in fact a Councillor of State under Primo de Rivera while being simultaneously general secretary of the UGT. Under the Franco dictatorship however the UGT was illegal as well and the main barrier to the CNT will probably prove to be the communist-controlled Workers' Commissions which grew up as a tolerated opposition within the regime's own trade union apparatus. (A fact pointing to further analogies between the communists of today and the social-democrats of yesteryear).

III

A number of factors might be adduced to explain how it was possible for the CNT to reorganise and then grow so quickly. The first point is that one result of the crisis of the sixties was the breakup of the conservative and authoritarian cold-war regimes in Western Europe and their replacement by broadly liberal or social-democratic regimes based on more extensive cooperation of unions and workers' parties with the state. (Eurocommunism is the left wing of this development). This is the process currently proceeding in Spain almost a decade later. One necessity for it is a "democratic" regime with freedom of political and trade union organisation. Thus for Spain to join the European Economic Community — or even just the "European Community" — the regime had to give up its compulsory corporative labour organisation and allow the parties to organise and contest elections. This liberalisation has allowed the CNT to reform. The regime could have decided to legalise all unions except the CNT and to maintain selective repression of anarcho-syndicalists but this would hardly have seemed important last year when the CNT was exceedingly small.[6] It is also possible that in the early period of the liberalisation the regime (or the U.S. or the Germans) wanted to allow the CNT to grow as a counter-weight to the well-established and communist-controlled Workers' Commissions which had originated in the early sixties as semi-legal bodies inside the official fascist vertical unions (with the assistance in some cases, it might be added, of the catholic clergy). However the possibility of reorganisation does not explain the sudden growth of the CNT in a situation in which the communist and ex-catholic unions have been quasi-legal, the German social-democrats have been pouring money into the UGT and the communists of course have had the money, middle-class support, staff and publications needed for building up the Workers' Commissions into a well-organised national union. If the CNT has re-emerged on a shoe-string budget with, as usual, no full-time organisers or officials and a semi-clandestine press, it must express rather deeper forces than those represented by the current international and domestic conjecture for the Spanish regime.

The next point is the peculiar age structure of the CNT. In general its membership is either under 35 or over 55 since a whole generation is missing today from Spanish politics. These are the people wose adolescence or childhood passed during the period of maximal repression and who had come to adulthood before the new developments — student unrest, worker unrest, the resurgence of regionalism, social catholicism and the echoes of the international movement — of the sixties. It is this generation that has voted the centre-right (the regime)* back into power and it will take years to develop political consciousness. The CNT is hence composed of a thin layer of old men[7] — usually ex-members or members emerging from clandestinity — and a much larger mass, perhaps 90 per cent of young people between 15 and 35. The current CNT is not to be explained as the remnants of the historical CNT.

It is beyond dispute that the existence of the CNT today is in fact the result of a decision by the small anarchist groups in Spain in the early seventies to reconstruct or recreate it. It is not a matter of the CNT just growing again around the nuclei represented by the handful of under-

* The silent generation of Spanish workers is said to have put Suarez in. But the socialists only got 5 per cent less than Suarez: 2½ per cent swing would have put them at the top of the poll. Is 2½ per cent a generation?

Also the working class parties' votes were as follows: socialists 29 per cent, C.P. 9 per cent, far left 2 per cent, total 40 per cent. Even not counting the abstentions, this must be close on the proportion of industrial and agricultural workers out of the population as a whole, the rest being made up of salesmen, clerks, servants, foremen, managers, bureaucrats, professionals, capitalists and farmers, not to mention clergy, police and army, all traditionally right wing. In other words, the 1977 election results could, unless there are other figures to prove it, have reflected class divisions, and there need have been no "crossing the line" by the silent generation. I must admit I don't know what proportion of the Spanish population consists of industrial and agricultural workers and their dependents, but I should be surprised if it were a majority; it certainly was not a majority in 1936. (After all, even in "industrialised" Germany in January 1933, the industrial workers voted solidly socialist or communist but were still swamped at the polls. (ed. note).

ground members of the older organisations still active once conditions became favourable. In general conditions have not been favourable. Rather there was a confluence between a tendency in the exile movement agitating for the reconstruction of the CNT, the skeletal CNT remaining in Spain and the much more numerous young anarchist groups originating inside the "authoritarian left" in the late sixties. Between 1970 and 1976 the "reconstruction" position became dominant in the clandestine anarchist groups and with the mushroom growth of the CNT since reorganisation it is only the most extremely anti-organisation or anti-unionist of the serious anarchist groups that remain outside. (There are however numerous groups of young anarchists on the fringes of the CNT). The CNT today is a mass organisation of anarchist youth even in Barcelona where its membership exceeds 10,000.

Thus to explain the growth of the CNT one must explain the libertarian tendency amongst Spanish youth and the syndicalist tendency in the working class. The second is the easier to do. The Spanish working class has had almost 40 years in the compulsory "vertical syndicates" — hierarchical structures by profession controlled from above by a fascist bureaucracy. Throughout this period the syndicates worked. as arms of the state, together with the employers. Thus the call for horizontal and democratic unions independent of the state and the employers must find an echo. All the new unions are at present formally agreed on this: the CNT differs only in calling for independence from political parties and by its much greater stress on the authority of the base and militant class struggle. This too finds its echo in the working class: despite — or, as some would have it, because of — the absence of unions there is a very high level of economic struggle in Spain which is being run directly by the workers themselves without the intermediation of union officials. This sort of activity fits perfectly into the conceptions of the CNT which then serves to publicise and generalise it.[8] It is possible too that with the myriad of political parties in Spain and their lack of a historical base of committed supporters on a mass scale, the CNT position of a union independent of the parties will also have its appeal and perhaps allow the CNT to make inroads into the "silent generation."

To some degree this analysis also answers the question as to a libertarian tendency: a syndicalism independent of state, employers and parties, based on rank and file democracy with revokable delegates and committees and aiming at the unification of all categories of workers within its ranks, is a libertarian syndicalism. However the CNT goes far beyond this; it still adheres to the full programme adopted at the last confederal congress in Saragossa in 1936 — proletarian revolution and libertarian communism. To join the CNT is to join an openly anarcho-syndicalist union with an explicitly anarchist goal. Why then does the CNT grow?

It does not help here to refer vaguely to the peculiarities of the latin temperament. The libertarian movement emerged in Spain and developed over a period of seventy years for quite definite reasons: social, economic and political. It was then destroyed by military and police force over a period of thirty years during which time the franquist regime proceeded with a general social, economic and political reconstruction that removed the libertarian movement's original bases. Anarchism had been a living force in Spain, by 1965 it was a dead one. One is observing today a second implantation of anarchism in Spain even if, once well under way, this implantation can also appear as a reconstruction or rediscovery.

The story of Spanish anarchism is sufficiently well known to give only the briefest sketch here. The Bakunist emissary Fanelli coming to Spain at a time (1868) of consideralbe political ferment found small groups of working class intellectuals in Madrid and Barcelona (precisely the skilled workers, usually printers, who would later be socialists) already interested in socio-political questions and belonging to the federalist movement of Pi y Margall which was influenced by Proudhon. In a series of meetings he succeeded in converting them to revolutionary socialism and the International and departing Spain left behind with them a small number of Bakunist texts, including the Statutes of the Alliance for Socialist Democracy, which spelt out the basic doctrine: atheism, materialism, socialism, revolutionary struggle against state and capital, independence from the (revolutionary) bourgeoisie. This they then spread to rural areas of the south, particularly Andalusia, where the country towns regularly became hotbeds of revolutionary ferment, and much more gradually and in a milder form to the partially unionised workers of Catalonia. With the foundation of the CNT in 1910 and the war-time take-off of Catalan industry anarcho-syndicalism became dominant in Barcelona and then through the south and east of Spain thus creating the classical worker-peasant basis of Spanish anarchism – the "anarchised" peasants of Andalusia and the Levante being sucked into the process of Catalan industrialisation and providing the raw material for both labour-intensive capital accumulation and the massive growth of revolutionary syndicalism in Barcelona. Later, in the 1930s, the CNT started to grow in the much less industrialised city of Madrid, previously a socialist stronghold, and to develop in the other regions of Spain. The overall trajectory however was from artisanal anarchism to rural anarchism to syndical anarchism and the fundamental social units in the spread and maintenance of anarchism were the small rural town and the union local.

The reasons that one must speak of a second implantation of anarchism will now be plain. The artisanal working class intelligentsia is no longer socially important; in any case it is miniscule by comparison with the radical student and ex-student intelligentsia. Rural Spain has been completely pacified and will not reawaken until entry to the European Economic Community (if this happens) shows up the antiquated nature of Spanish agriculture. And union locals, it goes without saying, have not existed for years. The rebirth of anarchism in Spain has been the result of different mechanisms.

IV

Once more we must return to the European crisis of the sixties and its repercussions in Spain. As has been mentioned this crisis was not only a crisis of capitalism but also of official communism. With certain qualifications one can date the renaissance of anarchism in the Anglo-European world from the crisis of the sixties. Particularly in the period 1968-72 a multitude of new anarchist groups, organisations and publications appeared — and usually disappeared; their members and readers being over-whelmingly young and often students. To cater to this potential market new editions of the classical anarchist writers started to appear in commercial publishers' lists and anarchism was suddenly once more "actuel." In Spain too a variety of anarchist and near-anarchist groups emerged during this period but the explosion of anarchist literature in Spain dates from 1975 and rather than being a mere reflex to the re-emergence of anarchism is part of the process of its development for in Spain the post-1968 anarchist movement has had a very different trajectory from that in the rest of the world.

Although the anarchist movement today is everywhere more extensive (and younger) than it was before 1968, the anarchist boom of 1968-72 nowhere led to the emergence of large scale organisations or even mass circulation publications. As a result many anarchists or potential anarchists passed on into the multitude of leninist, maoist and trotskyist groups springing up in the wake of 1968 or withdrew from political activity. In part this outcome was a product of youth and inexperience; in part a product of unfavourable conditions; in part also it was a result of the genuine difficulty of answering the question "What is to be done?" Historically the only answer to this question was that given by revolutionary syndicalism, but outside Spain and Argentina this had always only been a minority phenomenon and there were obvious difficulties for youth and student anarchists truing to do revolutionary work in well-established trade unions — let alone trying to found their own. Another fact to be noted here was that this new anarchism had emerged during the sixties in association with the general "youth culture" of that period, which had a number of implications for its relation to syndicalism. The first and most obvious is that the new anarchism was not a movement of the working class, not so much because of class origins (which were varied) as because of actual social location (students, unemployed, marginal workers). Secondly it often shared with the general youth culture a hostility to industry, science, cities (rather inconsistently!) and intellectual culture. In this way the new anarchism stood at the farthest possible distance from the old Spanish working class anarchism with its faith in science and labour. For the adherents of this youth cultural anarchism the advice "Into the factories!" was likely to be coolly received as indeed were any suggestions for serious and sustained activity.

In Spain however the situation was different since Spanish history supplied a relatively unambiguous answer to the question of activity and anarcho-syndicalism in Spain had a rich historical tradition to relate to and no really well-established reformist trade unions to block its growth. Small groups of theoretically minded anarchists were influenced by the anti-syndicalist ideologies adopted by post-1968 neo-anarchism from the Dutch and German left communists of the 1920s and 30s but i.i general the movement united around a syndicalist strategy. Thus in Spain the new anarchism has achieved a viable organisation. The CNT exists and all anarchists must define their positions with respect to it — or within it. Furthermore the CNT has its own political traditions even if these are more ambiguous than many people would like to believe.[9] A second problem of post-1968 anarchism — that of inexperience — is only now becoming a problem for the CNT with its mushroom growth. The groups and individuals who reformed the CNT were all experienced in the underground political and union struggle against the franquist regime, whether in the old CNT and underground, the clandestine anarchist groups or in the political organisations (socialist, communist, trotskyist, maoist or nationalist). This gave the new CNT a much large cadre of serious militants, trained in a much more serious school, than the whole of the European neo-anarchist groups put together. For these militants, many of whom have come from the parties, a return to them is not any solution. For those without such experience, joining the CNT for the first time and finding a majority as inexperienced as themselves (as is necessarily the case in the current phase of rapid growth), the experience will be undoubtedly disillusioning but for the moment the CNT mystique and the belief that in an organisation with real rank and file democracy things can be changed will probably hold them to the organisation. The problems for the CNT arise at a rather higher level than this and concern instead the problems of its political direction and membership composition.

V

In discussing anarchism in Spain today one must distinguish three key tendencies: the classical anarcho-syndicalist; the neo-anarchist (often also neo-marxist); the counter-cultural or neo-dadaist. The first is that of the old men of the underground and exile. The second is that of the clandestine groups originating in the late sixties and early seventies.[10] It is the third that best corresponds to the post-1968 movement in

Europe and Northern America. Whilst it is an important tendency in the ferment of cultural, sexual and intellectual liberation from franquism its significance for the CNT is mainly negative since its adherents can take a serious approach to neither industry nor the working class. In its pure form — represented by the important mass circulation Barcelona review *Ajoblanco* (White Garlic!) - it distinguishes itself sharply from the CNT.

This however does not mean that there are only two tendencies in the CNT. Even if one passes over the influence of the counter-culture on youth generally, and anarchist youth in particular,[11] the two key intellectual universes in the CNT do not give rise to two political tendencies. The reason for this is the persistence within Spanish anarchism of the old debate between anarchism and syndicalism or, to put it in the terminology of left-communism used by some of the marxist neo-anarchists, the issue of unitary organisation. The question is that of whether there should be a pure anarchist organisation — a resurrected Federacion Anarquista Iberica[12] — with the CNT being basically an industrial organisation pursuing the struggle in the economic sphere -- i.e. a pure, if radical, trade union — or whether the CNT alone can suffice for all forms of activity. Put differently it is also the question of whether a separately organised anarchist vanguard is required to lead the CNT ("in the moral sense" of course) or whether the CNT can be self-directing. Most precisely put it is the question of whether the division party/union, i.e. political organisation/economic organisation, must be accepted or whether a single mass organisation can embrace both aspects. Of course the issue is not always this clearly defined — for many young people it is more a matter of the romanticism of the super-radicalism of the FAI.

Closely related to this question of dual or unitary organisation is another: that of whether the CNT is an organisation for anarchists or for all workers and, further, whether "all workers" includes, members of political parties. In CNT circles this latter question is debated as the issue of "double militancy" and on this as on the question of the degree of ideological conviction required of a new member the different regional federations and syndicates differs.[13] A national plenum[14] of the CNT in 1976 resolved this issue by deciding that members of parties could not hold responsible positions in the CNT but the membership has increased by a factor of ten since then and the issue is of such importance that it will need a national conference to decide it. At present it mainly concerns the various trotskyist organisations entering the CNT, since the other left parties have their own unions or focus on the Workers Commissions or UGT, but this may change in the future.

Finally there is the question of the CNT's posture vis-a-vis the several reformist and revolutionary parties and, more particularly, their respective trade union organisations. On this question too there is a variation between the regions but the general rule would seem to be that at present joint action is only possible between the CNT and the unions to the left of the communist Workers' Commissions and between the CNT and the revolutionary organisations to the left of the main maoist and trotskyist parties although exceptions to this rule exist in the important centres of Barcelona, Valencia and Vizkaya. The CNT as a whole is committed to a policy of trans-union "workers' assemblies" on the job-site and pursues alliances with other unions and organisations on particular trade union and political issues. It has refused however to enter any permanent alliance restricting its freedom of action.

VI

With this we return to the general Spanish situation. It is of course no surprise that the government won the 15 June elections; the opposition parties had little time to build up elector loyalties or consciousness and the "democratisation" was a gift of the regime itself. The really interesting thing was the massive vote (29 per cent) for the Socialist Party,[15] the PSOE, which is, rather that the PCE, the historical party of the non-anarchist workers. Already the PSOE is seen as a future governing party, perhaps as early as the next elections. There is the strong possibility that it will pre-empt the social-reformist space that the PCE is currently vying for. If it can build up an apparatus to match the PCE's in size and effectiveness, the PCE will be permanently confined between the PSOE and its now legalised left-wing competitors who are pursuing more traditionally marxist and leninist policies.

There is then the question of the union movement. At present there are the union movements of the PSOE, PCE and the two maoist parties, ORT, and PTE; there is also the ex-catholic USO which inclines to the PSOE; there are regional ("nationalist") union centres in Catalonia and Euskadi close to the respective parties; finally there is the CNT. In total fewer than one million workers were in unions in May 1977. Of the unions the communist Workers' Commissions has the firmest base due to its long history of development inside the regime's now disbanded vertical syndicates. The CNT is probably the youngest since the "Unitary Syndicates" of the maoists were built around parties of several years standing. It is not clear however how such relative advantages and disadvantages will affect future developments. One logical block (which existed prior to May 1977) is that of the Workers' Commissions with the social-reformist UGT and USO, but the PSOE-UGT leadership may have strong reasons to maintain their own union. It would be likewise logical if the two maoist unions re-united but the political differences between the ORT and PTE which initially split their attempt at a single "unitary syndicate" to challenge the Workers' Commissions may continue to keep them apart. For the same reason an amalgamation between the Workers'

Commissions and the Unitary Syndicates seems out of the question. At present the Workers' Commissions are dominant in the industrial work-force but with the current low degree of unionisation and the uncertain prospects for the PCE it will not necessarily retain that position. A USO-UGT amalgamation could well become a majoritarian and a pole of attraction for as yet ununionised industrial workers.

If these are the chances for the formation of a reformist bloc what are those for a revolutionary bloc?

There is no doubt that at present the CNT must be the core of any revolutionary bloc. Despite its being smaller (in May 1977) than the claimed size of the maoist syndicates its ability to mobilise in the streets is considerably greater and its level of involvement in popular struggles is higher. It is perhaps more accurate to treat the CNT as the largest radical organisation than as the smallest of the major union centres. The question is whether the CNT can unite the other supposedly militant or radical unions togehter with it in economic and socio-political struggle. If this can be done in the long-term a shifting multi-union radical bloc may merge; if it cannot the CNT will be forced to attempt to rebuild its historical position as the radical union — a task that would necessitate not only the absorption of the militants of the maoist unions but also of the Workers' Commissions. At present this is far beyond the capacities of the CNT and nationally and in most regions the CNT is pursuing the tactic of a united front on the job through the slogan of 'workers' assemblies' and joint action with other organisations on specific issues (and on definite terms). In the course of this the CNT is establishing its public presence — an important step for an organisation barely eighteen months old, even if it bears a famous name.

Finally one must consider the interaction of the political and trade union sectors. Spain entered the elections with some 200 political parties and organisations; the new parliament contains only 7 significant ones. The left parties, unlike the Carillist PCE were not legalised for the elec-tions and so participated, if at all, in a variety of electoral fronts. If legalised they may have done better but even the fully legal, reasonably well financed and utterly respectable PCE only got 9 per cent of the vote. Hence for the trotskyist, maoist and left-communist militants, the question must be 'Where to now?'. A long-run consolidation of the PSOE may raise the same question for many PCE militants dissatisfied with the sacrifices (acceptance of the monarchy, franquist flag and armed forces) made for the elections. Such discontented militants would then drift fairly naturally to the CNT — particularly to a CNT not dominated by the younger (and older) anarchist intransigents. If so, the CNT could receive a second wave of trained militants on a larger scale which would allow it to recapture, if not a majoritarian position in the important regions, at least an unassailable minoritarian one.

It may well be that this is all that can be hoped for in the current phase of the European cycle. The "Spanish sixties" coincided not only with the death of Franco and transition to "democracy" but also with a general downturn in the European economy which was aggravated in Spain by a flight of fascist finance capital to Switzerland as a "strike" against democratisation. The European recovery will be felt in Spain but at present it is failing to increase employment and government action against the current 20 per cent rate of inflation may drive the unemployment rate beyond the current 5 per cent. The OECD report on Spain of June 1977 stresses the severe structural problems facing the economy and maps out a strategy of tight monetary policy together with fiscal policies to cushion the blow for low income earners. The latter, it admits, will probably require a full fiscal reform including general revision of taxation. Almost certainly the employers own strategy will be a continuing switch to capital-intensive methods of production, longer working hours and increased rates of exploitation – a reaction the OECD report already notes. Thus the unionisation of the Spanish working class will proceed under relatively conflictive conditions. This could mean the CNT established as the main, if still minoritarian, revolutionary organisation of the Spanish working class or it could mean a 'democratic-corporativist' reabsorption of the unions by the state apparatus along Western European lines which would leave the CNT as a pure anarchist opposition (as occurred with the syndicalists in Sweden). Other perspectives are also possible: a right-wing coup against a future left-wing government always remains a possibility in Spain, the countryside could reawaken or Catalonia redevelop a revolutionary working class.[16] Any of these developments would be profoundly de-stabilising and would perhaps favour the revolutionary left. Spain may yet again surprise Europe.

Footnotes

1. See his "Die Vorgeschichte der spanischen Revolution" of 1931 reprinted in *Karl Korsch : Politische Texte*, Frankfurt/M, 1974.
2. A replay in many ways justifies Marx's correction of Hegel on repetition in history: "the first time as tragedy, the second time as farce." Thus for instance this time the transition is not even to a democratic republic but merely to a constitutional monarchy (when it gets a constitution) and the Spanish Communist Party is no longer defending the bourgeois republic of the 1930s, but is rather attacking from what some wags have called a "socialist royalist" perspective, those leftists and others who want to restore it.

3. At the beginning of 1977 the PCE had some 120,000 members and rumours gave the much more underground revolutionary left parties perhaps some 6,000 - 8,000 a piece for the two major maoist parties and the major trotskyist party. The total membership of the 53 or more then illegal left organisations would hence be of.the order of 30,000 *excluding* the anarchists and anarcho-syndicalists. The recent elections which gave the PCE some 1,600,000 votes (around 9 per cent) throw little light on the question since most of the revolutionary left organisations — all of whom, unlike the PCE were still illegal — did not participate and the organisation of the elections greatly disadvantaged their various electoral fronts. In the next election one might expect them to receive several hundred thousand votes if they do not decay in the meanwhile.

4. In English one can read Miguel Garcia Garcia's *Franco's Prisoner* (Rupert Hart-Davis, London 1972) and Antonio Tellez's *Sabate : Guerrilla Extraordinary* (Cienfuegos Press, 1974). The anarchists had also been underground during the previous dictatorship of Primo de Rivera from 1923-30 and it would be interesting to compare their strategy and tactics then with those adopted in the 1939-50 period but very few works exist on either period.

5. This is the figure given by one of the liberal newspapers. The repression was so heavy that the demonstrators did not succeed in all gathering in one place at any stage during the day. However the writer saw two concentrations of a thousand or more and heard of others larger so the figure can probably be accepted.

6. Even at legalisation the CNT only had 5 per cent of the unionised workers if one accepts the possibly inflated figures of the other union centres.

7. One sees some old women as well but women seem to form a much larger, if still minority, proportion of the younger group.

8. It was the CNT's activity in two important "wildcat" strikes in Madrid and Barcelona that established its industrial presence in the current period.

9. The celebrated "anti-politicism" of the CNT was not only compatible with the "historic error" of entering the Caballero cabinet in 1936 but also with collaboration with all the military and political conspiracies against the Primo de Rivera dictatorship in the 1920s and the rather more dubiously useful political alliances of the CNT in exile in the 1940s.

10. The difference of these groups from the European ones of the same period lies in the fact that from the start they were necessarily underground and subject to heavy repression. Also in Spain, unlike the case in the rest of Europe, there was a concrete political task for revolutionary groups. Politically anarchist *groups* in Europe

covered the whole spectrum but the movement was more to its youth-cultural end.

11. It is surely no accident that the largest CNT event *ever* (excepting the funeral of Durruti) was the 1977 "cultural festival" in Barcelona.

12. The FAI was founded in 1927 to coordinate the clandestine anarchist movement more effectively and to fight against "reformist tendencies" in the CNT. After the emergence of the CNT from underground in 1930/31 the FAI succeeded in driving the oppositional pure "syndicalist" leaders out of the CNT and led the CNT onto a path of violent insurrectional and trade union struggles. The split with the opposition was healed in 1936 and after 1939 the FAI passed into exile. At present a number of anarchist groups in Spain are trying to reconstruct the FAI, but the government has so far prevented this by the arrest of the delegates at the first national meeting earlier this year. There is also an attempt to reorganise the anarchist youth organisation FIJL, and a much more successful and so far unrepressed attempt to reorganise the anarchist women's organisation, Mujeres Libres.

13. It is perhaps not surprising that maximal intolerance was achieved by the students of the law school section of the education syndicate in Madrid who resolved not only that no members of parties could belong to the CNT but also that all who argued for allowing double militancy should be expelled..

14. A meeting of mandated delegates of regions.

15. Premier Suarez's party, the Union Centro Democratica, itself only received 34 per cent. The PCE with some 9 per cent and the Alianza Popular (to the right of the UCD) with 8 per cent were well behind. The far left probably received some 2 per cent. Some 21 per cent of the electorate abstained, most probably because of indecision, but some in response to the abstention campaign of the far left, particualrly in Euskadi. Pre-election polls only predicted a hard-core abstention rate of 6 per cent.

16. The first signs of movement by small dairy farmers against their exploitation by big rural trading companies have already appeared in Aragon. A reawakening of the Catalan workers is more problematic, despite the evident popularity of the CNT there, because of the change of the industrial base since the 1930s. The only revolutionary working class in Spain at the moment is the Basque one.

The Debate on
Spanish Anarchism Today

Albert Meltzer

The great debate now going on in Spain's anarchist movement concerns the nature of libertarian organisation during a period of struggle. It is a pity that such a debate should be necessary, for it is all based upon a misconception of anarchism and anarcho-syndicalism. Understandably, the new generation does not know much about theory: how could it, after years of government genocide as a means of suppressing class war, during which the universal conspiracy of silence regarding anarchism was maintained, together with a policy of swift extermination of those who advocated it?

The movement in exile was bogged down in anti-fascist rhetoric which replaced libertarian thinking, and the need for cloaking itself in respectability so as to survive in a capitalist democracy. The debates that have gone on have been regarding the nature of democracy, anti-bolshevism, etc., and nothing at all — except in vague declamatory terms — about the problems the anarchist movement faced and should have to face.

Yet the moribund organisation which perpetuated this non-debate equally condemned the activists' struggle against fascism and so left the door open to bolshevism. One result is that the new generation has to think its way out afresh, and is going through the sterile ground familiar enough here but which ought not to be necessary in Spain where there has been factual experience of anarchist theory and practice — both in its strength and weakness. The debate is sometimes thought of as individualism versus "free communism" or "Anarchism" versus "Syndicalism" or the deficiencies or otherwise of the CNT when it is, in fact, a misconception of the whole idea itself, with the result that though the anarchists have the ball at their feet in Spain, they often do not know which game they are playing.

WHAT SHOULD BE THE C.N.T. ?

An anarcho-syndicalist organisation is a horizontal union body — as distinct from a vertical one. It is controlled not from the top down (nor even from the bottom up) but is controlled by all its membership. It is not a trade union with anarchist leadership — and to speak of it in the same breath as trade unionism is absurd, for the whole point of trade unionism is control from the top, which can integrate into any authoritarian system as well as democracy but never into one without the State. Trade unionism takes as its basic principle the closed shop, so that the fascist principle of the corporate state is what, inevitably, trade unionism must come to, in co-operation with employers' organisations and under the control of the State. Syndicalism is an advance on trade unionism, because its ideal is workers' control — i.e. workers' councils taking the means of production and the places of work into their own hands — but it too can be vertical rather than horizontal. The efforts by maoists and even trotskyists to set up their own unions in Spain are doomed to failure, for the believe in a party that "must" lead the masses who "of themselves have only a trade union consciousness;" hence they *want* unions composed of people less politically conscious than themselves and only taking orders. Such unions are better organised by socialists or communists. The "extreme left" can criticise other unions and fight against a backward leadership but is afraid of a setup where there is no leadership and its existence is superfluous.

It is a mistake many libertarians are making in Spain today to think that it is necessary to "make the CNT anarchist" — that if too many people enter into it it will "change its anarchist character," that it will become "purely syndicalist" and that this represents a menace. This only resolves itself into the problem of whether the CNT can remain horizontal or not. There is every sign that it *is* remaining horizontal. One does not want its committees to be composed of anarchists as if they were a vanguard party, over and above the non political mass.

The strike of the filling stations in Catalonia was the first test of the reconstructed CNT, now a minority union, unlike before the Civil War both because of the repression and the new industries. Because the other "big three" unions did not act in a militant fashion, due to the social contract made by their political representatives (not an unfamiliar situation to us), the CNT was able to push ahead with the strike, and it was brought to a more or less satisfactory conclusion. Strangely, this provoked great dissent among many anarchists some of whom felt — what then is the difference between the CNT and any trade union? Clearly, one strike cannot be "over the top into battle." The class struggle consist of small advances, sometimes retreats, then major advances, sometimes major retreats. There can be selling out by reformist or corrupt leaderships. But no leadership at all existed; and no sell out was therefore possible or performed. This is the stuff of what the CNT, that is to say horizontal union organisation, was and is all about. But is this revolutionary? There is no substitute for armed struggle. Industrial struggle is not that. Both have their place and time. Neither can be successful without the other.

From one article declaring "the CNT is sick", from a regional paper, I read with surprise that "what we want is a CNT able to organise the local communities, give support to housing ... ." and so on — rather than concentrate on industrial issues. It is not a "sickness" if a union organisation does not do what it is not intended to do. All those things should be done, some are being done, but they are part of a vast network of what is the libertarian movement and should not form part of the industrial organisation. The anarchist movement cannot be *solely* the CNT any more than the CNT can be solely anarchist. There are many ways of an anarcho-syndicalist movement operating: in the CNT today the various unions seem to form branches off the job and within the job form themselves into workers' councils, in which all workers, inclusive of those within other union centres, can join. Thus the apparent contradiction that a union representing one branch of workers can have some 500 members and bring 5000 out on strike.

In addition to the anarcho-syndicalist movement, however, it is urgent that the anarchist movement develops all the other facets of community work which are properly speaking not industrial at all. Revolution deoends upon the fact of change in the economy which will only be altered by a movement based on industry, and this is the first essential (but not the only essential) of social change; there are many other facets to revolutionary change as well. This was always recognised by the anarchist movement in the old days, with its Ferrer schools, its trade halls, its locals and centres, its libraries, its defence organisations, its newspapers, its fighting teams, in short a whole libertarian sub-structure which was in no way controlled by the CNT; and only part of which had anything to do with the FAI.

The enthusiasm expressed in earlier essays and articles on anarchism in Spain today is in no way abated. It is even more hopeful in Spain now than immediately preceding 1936, in some ways, for if the present situation were expressed in conflict it would show all the authoritarian parties, left or right, lined up against the workers. The pretence of their being anything else can deceive only those who want to be deceived. Spain, for better or worse, has become historically the forward line for anarchist ideas. If our ideas are to reach fulfilment, this forward line cannot be left without massive support from the rear.

Albert Meltzer

(Should you wish to make a financial contribution to the CNT you can do so by means of Mail Transfer from your account to that of Pedro Barrio Guazo, c.c. 8472, Banco Hispanoamericano, Oficina Urbana Lopez de Hoyos 126, Madrid 2, Spain. Correspondence to the National Committee of the CNT should be directed to Jose Elizalde, Apartado de Correos 150.105, Madrid, Spain. Exchange copies of all publications should be sent to the International Group at "Bicicleta", calle Pinilla del Valle, 1, Madrid 2, Spain.)